POLITICS AND ECONOMICS OF THE MIDDLE EAST

INTERNAL CONFLICT REGIONS IN THE MIDDLE EAST

IRAQ AND SYRIA

POLITICS AND ECONOMICS OF THE MIDDLE EAST

Additional books in this series can be found on Nova's website under the Series tab.

Additional e-books in this series can be found on Nova's website under the e-book tab.

POLITICS AND ECONOMICS OF THE MIDDLE EAST

INTERNAL CONFLICT REGIONS IN THE MIDDLE EAST

IRAQ AND SYRIA

DANA V. GRAY
EDITOR

New York

Copyright © 2014 by Nova Science Publishers, Inc.

All rights reserved. No part of this book may be reproduced, stored in a retrieval system or transmitted in any form or by any means: electronic, electrostatic, magnetic, tape, mechanical photocopying, recording or otherwise without the written permission of the Publisher.

For permission to use material from this book please contact us:
Telephone 631-231-7269; Fax 631-231-8175
Web Site: http://www.novapublishers.com

NOTICE TO THE READER

The Publisher has taken reasonable care in the preparation of this book, but makes no expressed or implied warranty of any kind and assumes no responsibility for any errors or omissions. No liability is assumed for incidental or consequential damages in connection with or arising out of information contained in this book. The Publisher shall not be liable for any special, consequential, or exemplary damages resulting, in whole or in part, from the readers' use of, or reliance upon, this material. Any parts of this book based on government reports are so indicated and copyright is claimed for those parts to the extent applicable to compilations of such works.

Independent verification should be sought for any data, advice or recommendations contained in this book. In addition, no responsibility is assumed by the publisher for any injury and/or damage to persons or property arising from any methods, products, instructions, ideas or otherwise contained in this publication.

This publication is designed to provide accurate and authoritative information with regard to the subject matter covered herein. It is sold with the clear understanding that the Publisher is not engaged in rendering legal or any other professional services. If legal or any other expert assistance is required, the services of a competent person should be sought. FROM A DECLARATION OF PARTICIPANTS JOINTLY ADOPTED BY A COMMITTEE OF THE AMERICAN BAR ASSOCIATION AND A COMMITTEE OF PUBLISHERS.

Additional color graphics may be available in the e-book version of this book.

Library of Congress Cataloging-in-Publication Data

ISBN: 978-1-63321-259-6

Published by Nova Science Publishers, Inc. † *New York*

CONTENTS

Preface		**vii**
Chapter 1	Iraq: Politics, Governance, and Human Rights *Kenneth Katzman*	**1**
Chapter 2	Armed Conflict in Syria: Overview and U.S. Response *Christopher M. Blanchard, Carla E. Humud* *and Mary Beth D. Nikitin*	**65**
Chapter 3	Syria: Overview of the Humanitarian Response *Rhoda Margesson and Susan G. Chesser*	**99**
Index		**137**

PREFACE

Since the 2011 U.S. withdrawal from Iraq, sectarian divisions have widened, fueling a revival of a Sunni Muslim insurgent challenge to Iraq's stability. Iraq's Sunni Arab Muslims resent Shiite political domination and perceived discrimination by the government of Prime Minister Nuri al-Maliki. Iraq's Kurds are embroiled in separate political disputes with the Baghdad government over territorial, political, and economic issues, particularly their intent to separately export large volumes of oil produced in the Kurdish region. Fighting also continues across Syria, pitting government forces and their foreign allies against a range of anti-government insurgents, some of whom also are fighting amongst themselves. The ongoing conflict that began in March 2011 in Syria has created one of the most pressing humanitarian crises in the world. Three years later, as of early March 2014, an estimated 9.3 million people inside Syria, nearly half the population, have been affected by the conflict. This book discusses the political, and internal conflicts of both Iraq and Syria. It provides information on the politics, governance, and human rights in Iraq; an overview of armed conflict in Syria, as well as the United States response; and an overview of the humanitarian response in Syria as well.

Chapter 1 – Since the 2011 U.S. withdrawal from Iraq, sectarian divisions have widened, fueling a revival of a Sunni Muslim insurgent challenge to Iraq's stability. Iraq's Sunni Arab Muslims resent Shiite political domination and perceived discrimination by the government of Prime Minister Nuri al-Maliki. Iraq's Kurds are embroiled in separate political disputes with the Baghdad government over territorial, political, and economic issues, particularly their intent to separately export large volumes of oil produced in the Kurdish region. The political rifts produced a significant and sustained uprising in December 2013 led by the Sunni insurgent group Al Qaeda in Iraq, now also known by the name Islamic State of Iraq and the Levant (ISIL). The group and its allies still control several cities in Anbar Province, including the key city of Fallujah, and have pockets of control near Baghdad. There are a growing number of reports that some Shiite militias have reactivated to retaliate for violence against Shiites. The sectarian rift and violence, which killed nearly 9,000 Iraqis in 2013 (double the figure for 2012), could affect the legitimacy of national elections for a new parliament and government set for April 30, 2014. Facing divided opponents, Maliki is widely expected to seek to retain his post after that vote, largely on the strength of Shiite voters who see him as standing up to the Sunni challenge.

The latest violence has exposed weaknesses in the 800,000 person Iraqi Security Forces (ISF) in the absence of direct U.S. military involvement in Iraq. The ISF and informal security structures put in place during the U.S. intervention in Iraq in 2003-2011 have faltered against the ISIL challenge. Some formerly pro-government Sunni fighters have joined the uprising, further weakening government attempts to suppress the uprising.

Chapter 2 – Fighting continues across Syria, pitting government forces and their foreign allies against a range of anti-government insurgents, some of whom also are fighting amongst themselves. Since March 2011, the conflict has driven more than 2.6 million Syrians into neighboring countries as refugees (out of a total population of more than 22 million). Millions more Syrians are internally displaced and in need of humanitarian assistance, of which the United States remains the largest bilateral provider, with more than $1.7 billion in funding identified to date. U.S. nonlethal assistance to opposition forces was placed on hold in December 2013, as fighting in northern Syria disrupted mechanisms put in place to monitor and secure U.S. supplies. Administration officials have since resumed some assistance to select opposition groups.

Neither pro-Asad forces nor their opponents appear capable of consolidating their battlefield gains in Syria or achieving outright victory there in the short term. Improved coordination among some anti-government forces and attrition in government ranks make a swift reassertion of state control over all of Syria unlikely. Conflict between the Islamic State of Iraq and the Levant (ISIL, a.k.a. ISIS) and other anti-Asad forces has intensified. The war in Syria is exacerbating local sectarian and political conflicts within Lebanon and Iraq, threatening national stability.

Chapter 3 – The ongoing conflict that began in March 2011 in Syria has created one of the most pressing humanitarian crises in the world. Three years later, as of early March 2014, an estimated 9.3 million people inside Syria, nearly half the population, have been affected by the conflict. It is estimated that there are 6.5 million displaced persons inside Syria and 2.5 million Syrians displaced as refugees, with 97% fleeing to countries in the immediate surrounding region, including Turkey, Lebanon, Jordan, Iraq, Egypt, and other parts of North Africa. The situation is fluid and continues to worsen, while humanitarian needs are immense and increase daily.

While internationally supervised disarmament of chemical weapons in Syria is proceeding, albeit with some difficulty, U.S. and international diplomatic efforts to negotiate a political end to the fighting in Syria opened on January 22, 2014, in Montreux, Switzerland. The "Geneva II" talks include some members of the Syrian opposition, representatives of the Syrian government, and other government leaders. The first round of talks came to an end on January 31 and resumed February 10-15, but ended with little progress in efforts to end the civil war. The parties reportedly agreed to an agenda for a third round of talks. Many experts and observers hoped that a lasting agreement would have been reached on "humanitarian pauses" to allow access and relief to thousands of civilians blockaded in towns and cities in Syria. On February 22, the U.N. Security Council unanimously adopted Resolution 2139 (2014) to increase humanitarian access and aid delivery in Syria.

In: Internal Conflict Regions in the Middle East   ISBN: 978-1-63321-259-6
Editor: Dana V. Gray   © 2014 Nova Science Publishers, Inc.

Chapter 1

IRAQ: POLITICS, GOVERNANCE, AND HUMAN RIGHTS*

Kenneth Katzman

SUMMARY

Since the 2011 U.S. withdrawal from Iraq, sectarian divisions have widened, fueling a revival of a Sunni Muslim insurgent challenge to Iraq's stability. Iraq's Sunni Arab Muslims resent Shiite political domination and perceived discrimination by the government of Prime Minister Nuri al-Maliki. Iraq's Kurds are embroiled in separate political disputes with the Baghdad government over territorial, political, and economic issues, particularly their intent to separately export large volumes of oil produced in the Kurdish region. The political rifts produced a significant and sustained uprising in December 2013 led by the Sunni insurgent group Al Qaeda in Iraq, now also known by the name Islamic State of Iraq and the Levant (ISIL). The group and its allies still control several cities in Anbar Province, including the key city of Fallujah, and have pockets of control near Baghdad. There are a growing number of reports that some Shiite militias have reactivated to retaliate for violence against Shiites. The sectarian rift and violence, which killed nearly 9,000 Iraqis in 2013 (double the figure for 2012), could affect the legitimacy

---

* This is an edited, reformatted and augmented version of a Congressional Research Service publication RS21968, prepared for Members and Committees of Congress dated April 23, 2014.

of national elections for a new parliament and government set forApril 30, 2014. Facing divided opponents, Maliki is widely expected to seek to retain his post after that vote, largely on the strength of Shiite voters who see him as standing up to the Sunni challenge.

The latest violence has exposed weaknesses in the 800,000 person Iraqi Security Forces (ISF) in the absence of direct U.S. military involvement in Iraq. The ISF and informal security structures put in place during the U.S. intervention in Iraq in 2003-2011 have faltered against the ISIL challenge. Some formerly pro-government Sunni fighters have joined the uprising, further weakening government attempts to suppress the uprising.

U.S. forces left in December 2011 in keeping with a November 2008 bilateral U.S.-Iraq Security Agreement. Iraq had refused to extend their presence, seeking to put behind it the period of U.S. political and military control. Program components of what were to be enduring, close security relations languished, including U.S. training for Iraq's security forces through an Office of Security Cooperation—Iraq (OSC-I) and a State Department police development program. U.S. arms sales continued and have expanded somewhat to help Iraq confront the Sunni/ISIL uprising. The United States has accelerated delivery of HELLFIRE missiles and surveillance systems, and will soon begin deliveries of F-16 combat aircraft, air defense equipment, and attack helicopters. The Administration has ruled out any reintroduction of U.S. ground troops to Iraq, even if the Iraqi government were to request them. At the same time, the United States has counseled Iraqi restraint in use of force against civilians and promoted dialogue among Iraqi factions to resolve the underlying sources of Sunni resentment.

The Administration and Congress continue to cultivate Iraq as an ally in part to preserve the legacy of the U.S intervention and to prevent Iraq from falling under the sway of Iran. Asserting that the Sunni-led rebellion in Syria is emboldening Iraqi Sunnis, Maliki has not joined U.S. and other Arab state calls for Syrian President Bashar Al Assad to leave office and Iraq has not consistently sought to prevent Iranian overflights of arms deliveries to Syria. Still, the legacy of the 1980-1988 Iran-Iraq war, Arab and Persian differences, and Iraq's efforts to reestablish its place in the Arab world limit Iranian influence over the Baghdad government. Iraq took a large step toward returning to the Arab fold by hosting an Arab League summit on March 27-29, 2012, and has substantially repaired relations with Kuwait, the state that Saddam Hussein invaded in 1990. In June 2013, the relationship with Kuwait helped Iraq emerge from most Saddam-era restrictions imposed under Chapter VII of the U.N. Charter.

OVERVIEW OF THE POST-SADDAM POLITICAL TRANSITION

A U.S.-led military coalition, in which about 250,000 U.S. troops participated, crossed the border from Kuwait into Iraq on March 19, 2003. Turkey refused to allow any of the coalition force to move into Iraq from the north. After several weeks of combat, the regime of Saddam Hussein fell on April 9, 2003. During the 2003-2011 presence of U.S. forces, Iraq completed a transition from the dictatorship of Saddam Hussein to a plural political system in which varying sects and ideological and political factions compete in elections. A series of elections began in 2005, after a one-year occupation period and a subsequent seven-month interim period of Iraqi self-governance that gave each community a share of power and prestige to promote cooperation and unity. Still, disputes over the relative claim of each community on power and economic resources permeated almost every issue in Iraq and were never fully resolved. These unresolved differences—muted during the last years of the U.S. military presence—reemerged in mid-2012 and have returned Iraq to sectarian conflict.

Initial Transition and Construction of the Political System

After the fall of Saddam's regime, the United States set up an occupation structure based on concerns that immediate sovereignty would favor established Islamist and pro-Iranian factions over nascent pro-Western secular parties. In May 2003, President Bush named Ambassador L. Paul Bremer to head a "Coalition Provisional Authority" (CPA), which was recognized by the United Nations as an occupation authority. In July 2003, Bremer ended Iraqi transition negotiations and appointed a non-sovereign Iraqi advisory body, the 25-member "Iraq Governing Council" (IGC). U.S. and Iraqi negotiators, advised by a wide range of international officials and experts, drafted a "Transitional Administrative Law" (TAL, interim constitution), which became effective on March 4, 2004.[1] On June 28, 2004, after about one year of occupation, Ambassador Bremer appointed an Iraqi interim government, meeting the TAL-specified deadline of June 30, 2004, for the end of the occupation period. The TAL also laid out a 2005 elections roadmap.

Major Factions Dominate Post-Saddam Politics

The interim government was headed by a prime minister, Iyad al-Allawi, and a president, Sunni tribalist Ghazi al-Yawar. It was heavily populated by parties and factions that had long campaigned to oust Saddam, including the Shiite Islamist parties called the Da'wa Party and the Islamic Supreme Council of Iraq (ISCI). Both of these parties were Iran-supported underground movements that worked to overthrow Saddam Hussein since the early 1980s. Allawi led the Iraq National Accord (INA), a secular, non-sectarian anti-Saddam faction. Allawi is a Shiite Muslim but his supporters are mostly Sunni Arabs, including some former members of the Baath Party.

- *Da'wa Party "State of Law Coalition."* The largest faction of the Da'wa Party is led by Nuri al-Maliki, who displaced former leader Ibrahim al-Jaafari in 2006. Da'wa was active against Saddam but also had operatives in some Persian Gulf states, including Kuwait, where they committed attacks against the ruling family during the 1980s. Da'wa is the core of Maliki's current "State of Law" election coalition.
- *Islamic Supreme Council of Iraq* (ISCI) is led by the Hakim family— the sons of the revered late Grand Ayatollah Muhsin Al Hakim, who hosted Iran's Ayatollah Ruhollah Khomeini when he was in exile in Iraq during 1964-1978. In the immediate post-Saddam period, Abd al-Aziz al-Hakim led the group after the August 2003 assassination of his elder brother, Mohammad Baqr al-Hakim, in a bombing outside a Najaf mosque. After Abd al-Aziz al-Hakim's death in August 2009, his son Ammar, born in 1971, succeeded him as ISCI chief.
- *Sadrists.* Another Shiite Islamist faction, one loyal to radical cleric Moqtada Al Sadr, whose family had lived under Saddam's rule, gelled as a cohesive party after Saddam's ouster and also formed an armed faction called the Mahdi Army. Sadr is the son of revered Ayatollah Mohammad Sadiq Al Sadr, who was killed by Saddam's security forces in 1999, and a relative of Mohammad Baqr Al Sadr, a Shiite theoretician and contemporary and colleague of Ayatollah Khomeini. The Sadrists compete in elections under the "Al Ahrar" (Liberal) banner.
- *Kurdish Factions: KDP and PUK.* Also influential in post-Saddam politics in Baghdad are the long-established Kurdish parties the Kurdistan Democratic Party (KDP) headed by Masoud Barzani, son of the late, revered Kurdish independence fighter Mullah Mustafa

Barzani, and the Patriotic Union of Kurdistan (PUK) headed by Jalal Talabani. Barzani's brother, Idris, was killed during the 1980-88 Iran-Iraq war; Idris's son, Nechirvan, is a senior figure in Kurdish governance.

- *Iraqi National Congress* (INC). Another significant longtime anti-Saddam faction was the INC of Ahmad Chalabi. The group had lobbied extensively in Washington, DC, since the early 1990s for the United States to overthrow Saddam, but did poorly in post-Saddam Iraqi elections.
- *Iraqi National Alliance* (INA)/*Iraqiyya*. Another major exile group that became prominent in post-Saddam Iraq was the Iraqi National Alliance (INA) of Iyad al-Allawi. Allawi is a Shiite but most of his political allies are Sunni Arab. After returning to Iraq, Allawi went on to become prime minister of the interim government and then leader of the major anti-Maliki secular bloc now called *"Iraqiyya."*

Interim Government Formed and New Coalitions Take Shape

Iraqi leaders of all factions agreed that elections should determine the composition of Iraq's new power structure. The beginning of the elections process was set for 2005 to produce a transitional parliament that would supervise writing a new constitution, a public referendum on a new constitution, and then the election of a full-term government under that constitution.

In accordance with the dates specified in the TAL, the first post-Saddam election was held on January 30, 2005, for a 275-seat transitional National Assembly (which would form an executive), four-year-term provincial councils in all 18 provinces ("provincial elections"), and a Kurdistan regional assembly (111 seats). The Assembly election was conducted according to the "proportional representation/closed list" election system, in which voters chose among "political entities" (a party, a coalition of parties, or people). The ballot included 111 entities, 9 of which were multi-party coalitions. Still restive, Sunni Arabs (20% of the overall population) boycotted, winning only 17 Assembly seats, and only 1 seat on the 51-seat Baghdad provincial council. Moqtada Al Sadr, whose armed faction was then fighting U.S. forces, also boycotted the election. The resulting transitional government included PUK leader Jalal Talabani as president and then Da'wa party leader Ibrahim al-Jafari as prime minister. Sunni Arabs held the posts of Assembly speaker, deputy president, one of the deputy prime ministers, and six ministers, including defense.

Kenneth Katzman

Permanent Constitution[2]

A major task accomplished by the elected transitional Assembly was the drafting of a permanent constitution, adopted in a public referendum of October 15, 2005. A 55-member drafting committee in which Sunnis were underrepresented produced a draft providing for:

- The three Kurdish-controlled provinces of Dohuk, Irbil, and Sulaymaniyah to constitute a legal "region" administered by the Kurdistan Regional Government (KRG), which would have its own elected president and parliament (Article 113).
- a December 31, 2007, deadline to hold a referendum on whether Kirkuk (Tamim province) would join the Kurdish region (Article 140).
- designation of Islam as "a main source" of legislation.
- all orders of the CPA to be applicable until amended (Article 126), and a "Federation Council" (Article 62), a second chamber with size and powers to be determined in future law (not adopted to date).
- a 25% electoral goal for women (Article 47).
- families to choose which courts to use for family issues (Article 41); making only primary education mandatory (Article 34).
- Islamic law experts and civil law judges to serve on the federal supreme court (Article 89). Many Iraqi women opposed this and the previous provisions as giving too much discretion to male family members.
- two or more provinces to join together to form new autonomous "regions." This provision was implemented by an October 2006 law on formation of regions.
- "regions" to organize internal security forces, legitimizing the fielding of the Kurds' *peshmerga* militia (Article 117). This continued a TAL provision.
- the central government to distribute oil and gas revenues from "current fields" in proportion to population, and for regions to have a role in allocating revenues from new energy discoveries (Article 109).

These provisions left many disputes unresolved, particularly the balance between central government and regional and local authority. The TAL made approval of the constitution subject to a veto if a two-thirds majority of voters in any three provinces voted it down. Sunnis registered in large numbers (70%-85%) to try to defeat the constitution, despite a U.S.-mediated agreement of October 11, 2005, to have a future vote on amendments to the constitution. The Sunni provinces of Anbar and Salahuddin had a 97% and 82% "no" vote, respectively, but the constitution was adopted because Nineveh province voted 55% "no"—short of the two-thirds "no" majority needed to vote the constitution down.

December 15, 2005, Elections Establish the First Full-Term Goverment

The December 15, 2005, elections were for a full-term (four-year) national government (also in line with the schedule laid out in the TAL). Each province contributed a set number of seats to a "Council of Representatives" (COR), a formula adopted to attract Sunni participation. There were 361 political "entities," including 19 multi-party coalitions, competing in a "closed list" voting system (in which votes are cast only for parties and coalitions, not individual candidates). Voters chose lists representing their sects and regions, and the Shiites and Kurds again emerged dominant. The COR was inaugurated on March 16, 2006, but political infighting caused the replacement of Jafari with another Da'wa figure, Nuri Kamal al-Maliki, as Prime Minister.

On April 22, 2006, the COR approved Talabani to continue as president. His two deputies were Adel Abd al-Mahdi (incumbent) of ISCI and Tariq al-Hashimi, leader of the mostly Sunni Iraqi Islamic Party (IIP). Another Sunni figure, Mahmoud Mashhadani, became COR speaker. Maliki won COR approval of a 37-member cabinet on May 20, 2006. Of the 37 posts, there were 19 Shiites; 9 Sunnis; 8 Kurds; and 1 Christian. Four were women.

2006-2011: SECTARIAN CONFLICT AND U.S.-ASSISTED RECONCILIATION

The Bush Administration deemed the 2005 elections successful, but they did not resolve the Sunni-Arab grievances over their diminished positions in the power structure. Subsequent events worsened the violence by exposing and reinforcing the political weakness of the Sunni Arabs. With tensions high, the bombing of a major Shiite shrine within the Sunni-dominated province of Salahuddin in February 2006 set off major sectarian unrest, characterized in part by Sunni insurgent activities against government and U.S. troops, high-casualty suicide and other bombings, and the growth of Shiite militia factions to counter the Sunni acts. The sectarian violence was so serious that many experts, by the end of 2006, were considering the U.S. mission as failing - an outcome that an "Iraq Study Group" concluded was a significant possibility absent a major change in U.S. policy.[3]

As assessments of possible overall U.S. policy failure multiplied, the Administration and Iraq agreed in August 2006 on a series of "benchmarks" that, if adopted and implemented, might achieve political reconciliation. Under Section 1314 of a FY2007 supplemental appropriation (P.L. 110-28), "progress" on 18 political and security benchmarks—as assessed in Administration reports due by July 15, 2007, and then September 15, 2007— was required for the United States to provide $1.5 billion in Economic Support Funds (ESF) to Iraq. President Bush exercised the waiver provision. The law also mandated an assessment by the Government Accountability Office, by September 1, 2007, of Iraqi performance on the benchmarks, as well as an outside assessment of the Iraqi security forces (ISF).

UNITED NATIONS ASSISTANCE MISSION – IRAQ (UNAMI)

The United Nation contributed to political reconciliation through its U.N. Assistance Mission—Iraq (UNAMI). The head of UNAMI is also the Special Representative of the Secretary General for Iraq. The first head of the office was killed in a car bombing on his headquarters in August 2003. Ad Melkert was the UNAMI head during 2009-2011. He was replaced in September 2011 by Martin Kobler, who was replaced by Bulgarian diplomat Nickolay Mladenov in September 2013. The mandate of UNAMI was established in 2003 and U.N. Security Council Resolution 2110 of July 24, 2013 provided the latest yearly renewal (until July 31, 2014). UNAMI's primary activities have been to help build civil society, assist vulnerable populations, consult on possible solutions to the Arab-Kurd dispute over Kirkuk province (see below), and resolve the status of the Iranian opposition group People's Mojahedin Organization of Iran that remains in Iraq (see below).

In early 2007, the United States began a "surge" of about 30,000 additional U.S. forces (bringing U.S. troop levels from their 2004-2006 baseline of about 138,000 to about 170,000) in order to blunt insurgent momentum and take advantage of growing Sunni Arab rejection of extremist groups. The Administration cited as partial justification for the surge the Iraq Study Group's recommendation of such a step. As 2008 progressed, citing the achievement of many of the major Iraqi legislative benchmarks and a dramatic drop in sectarian violence, the Bush Administration asserted that political reconciliation was advancing. However, U.S. officials maintained that the extent and durability of the reconciliation would depend on implementation of adopted laws, on further compromises among ethnic groups, and on continuing reductions in levels of violence.

Iraqi Governance Strengthens as Sectarian Conflict Abates

The passage of Iraqi laws in 2008 that were considered crucial to reconciliation, continued reductions in violence accomplished by the U.S. surge, and the Sunni militant turn away from violence facilitated political stabilization. A March 2008 offensive ordered by Maliki against the Sadr faction and other militants in Basra and environs ("Operation Charge of the Knights") pacified the city and caused many Sunnis and Kurds to see Maliki as willing to take on armed groups even if they were Shiite. This contributed to a decision in July 2008 by several Sunni ministers to end a one-year boycott of the cabinet.

Empowering Local Governance: 2008 Provincial Powers Law (Law No. 21)

In 2008, a "provincial powers law" (Law Number 21) was adopted to decentralize governance by delineating substantial powers for provincial (governorate) councils. It replaced a 1969 Provinces Law (Number 159). Under the 2008 law, the provincial councils enact provincial legislation, regulations, and procedures, and choose the province's governor and two deputy governors. The provincial administrations draft provincial budgets and implement federal policies. Some central government funds are given as grants directly to provincial administrations for their use. The term of the provincial councils is four years from the date of their first convention.

Since enactment, Law 21 has been used on several occasions to try to pacify restive areas of Iraq. Law 21 was amended substantially in late June 2013 to give the provincial governments substantially more power, a move intended to satisfy Sunnis. As a consequence of that and other laws, provinces have a greater claim on Iraqi financial resources than do districts, and many communities that dominate specific areas support converting their areas into provinces. In December 2013, the government decided to convert the district of Halabja—a symbolic city to the Kurds because of Saddam's use of chemical weapons there in 1988—into a separate province. On January 21, 2014, the government announced it had decided to convert several districts into new provinces: Fallujah (in Anbar Province), a hotbed of Sunni restiveness; Tuz Khurmato (in Salahuddin Province) and Tal Affar (in Nineveh Province), which both have Turkmen majorities; and the Nineveh Plains (also in Nineveh), which has a mostly Assyrian Christian population. This latter announcement came amid a major Sunni uprising in Anbar Province, discussed below, and appeared clearly intended to keep minorities and Sunnis on the side of the Maliki government.

2009 Provincial Elections. After the 2008 provincial powers law was enacted, the next set of provincial elections were planned for October 1, 2008. They were postponed when Kurdish opposition caused a presidential veto of a July 22, 2008 draft election law that provided for equal division of power in Kirkuk (among Kurds, Arabs, and Turkomans)—a proposal that would have diluted Kurdish dominance there. On September 24, 2008, the COR passed another election law, providing for the provincial elections by January 31, 2009, but putting off provincial elections in Kirkuk and the three KRG provinces. In the elections, about 14,500 candidates vied for the 440 provincial council seats in the 14 Arab-dominated provinces of Iraq. About 4,000 of the candidates were women. About 17 million Iraqis (any Iraqi 18 years of age or older) were eligible for the vote, which was run by the Iraqi Higher Election Commission (IHEC). Pre-election violence was minimal. Turnout was about 51%, somewhat lower than some expected.

The certified vote totals (March 29, 2009) gave Maliki's "State of Law Coalition" (a coalition composed of his Da'wa Party plus other mostly Shiite allies) a clear victory with 126 out of the 440 seats available (28%). ISCI went from 200 council seats to only 50, a result observers attributed to its perceived close ties to Iran and its corruption. Iyad al-Allawi's faction won 26 seats, a gain of eight seats, and a competing Sunni faction loyal to Tariq al-Hashimi won 32 seats, a loss of about 15. Sunni tribal leaders, who were widely credited for turning Iraqi Sunnis against Al Qaeda-linked extremists in Iraq, had boycotted the 2005 elections but participated in the 2009 elections. Their slate came in first in Anbar Province. Although Maliki's State of Law coalition fared well, his party still needed to strike bargains with rival factions to form provincial administrations. Subsequent provincial elections in Arab-dominated provinces were held during April-June 2013, as discussed below.

The March 7, 2010, Elections: Shiites Fracture and Sunnis Cohere

After a strong showing for his list in the provincial elections, Maliki was favored to retain his position in the March 7, 2010, COR elections that would choose the next government. Maliki derived further political benefit from the U.S. implementation of the U.S.-Iraq "Security Agreement" (SA), discussed below. Yet, as 2009 progressed, Maliki's image as protector of law and order was tarnished by several high-profile attacks, including major bombings in Baghdad on August 20, 2009, in which almost 100 Iraqis were killed and the buildings housing the Ministry of Finance and of Foreign Affairs were heavily damaged. As Maliki's image of strong leadership faded that year, Shiite unity broke down and a strong rival Shiite slate took shape—the "Iraqi National Alliance (INA)" consisting of ISCI, the Sadrists, and other Shiite figures. The INA coalition believed that each of its component factions would draw support from their individual constituencies to produce an election victory.

To Sunni Arabs, the outwardly cross-sectarian Iraq National Movement ("Iraqiyya") of former transitional Prime Minister Iyad al-Allawi (a broader coalition than his INA faction) had strong appeal. There was an openly Sunni slate, leaning Islamist, called the Accordance, and some Sunni figures joined Shiite slates in order to improve their chances of winning a seat.

Election Law and "De-Baathification" Controversies

The 2010 election was clouded by several disputes over election rules and procedures. Under the Iraqi constitution, the elections were to be held by January 31, 2010, in order to allow 45 days before the March 15, 2010, expiry of the COR's term. The election laws that run the election and can shape the election outcome were the subject of disputes, and the COR repeatedly missed self-imposed deadlines to pass them. Many COR members leaned toward a closed list system, but those who wanted an open list vote (allowing voters to vote for candidates as well as coalition slates) prevailed. Sunnis lost their struggle to have "reserved seats" for Iraqis in exile; many Sunnis had gone into exile after the fall of Saddam Hussein. Each province served as a single constituency (see **Table 3** for the number of seats per province).

The version of the election law passed by the COR on November 8, 2009 (141 out of 195 COR deputies voting), expanded the size of the COR to 325 total seats. Of these, 310 were allocated by province, with the constituency sizes ranging from Baghdad's 68 seats to Muthanna's seven. The COR size, in the absence of a recent census, was based on taking 2005 population figures and adding 2.8% per year growth.[4] The remaining 15 seats were to be minority reserved seats (8) and "compensatory seats" (7)—seats allocated from "leftover" votes for parties and slates that did not meet a minimum threshold to win any seat.

Table 1. Major Coalitions for 2010 National Elections

State of Law Coalition (slate no. 337)	Led by Maliki and his Da'wa Party. Included some Sunni leaders such as Shaykh Hatim al-Dulaymi. Appealed to Shiite sectarianism during the campaign by backing the exclusion of candidates with links to outlawed Baath Party.
Iraqi National Alliance (slate no. 316)	Formed in August 2009, was the most formidable challenger to Maliki's slate. Consisted mainly of his Shiite competitors, including ISCI, the Sadrist movement, the Fadilah Party, the Iraqi National Congress of Ahmad Chalabi, and the faction of ex-Prime Minister Ibrahim al-Jafari.
Iraqiyya (slate no. 333)	Formed in October 2009 by former Prime Minister Iyad al-Allawi, who is Shiite, although his faction is mainly Sunni, and Sunni leader Saleh al-Mutlaq (ex-Baathist leader of the National Dialogue Front). The coalition included the IIP and several powerful Sunni individuals, including Usama al-Nujaifi and Rafi al-Issawi.
Kurdistan Alliance (slate no. 372)	Competed again as a joint KDP-PUK Kurdish list. However, Kurdish solidarity was shaken by July 25, 2009, Kurdistan elections in which a breakaway PUK faction called Change (Gorran) did unexpectedly well. Gorran ran its own separate list for the March 2010 elections.
Unity Alliance of Iraq (slate no. 348)	Led by Interior Minister Jawad Bolani, a moderate Shiite, and included the Sunni tribal faction of Shaykh Ahmad Abu Risha, brother of slain leader of the Sunni Awakening movement in Anbar. The list also included first post-Saddam defense minister Sadun al-Dulaymi.
Iraqi Accordance (slate no. 338)	A coalition of Sunni parties, including some breakaway leaders of the IIP. Led by Ayad al-Samarrai, then-speaker of the COR.

Sources: Carnegie Endowment for International Peace; various press.

Iraq: Politics, Governance, and Human Rights

De-Baathification Candidate Vetting. The 2010 electoral process was at least partly intended to bring Sunni Arabs further into the political structure. That goal was jeopardized by a major dispute over candidate eligibility. In January 2010, the Justice and Accountability Commission (JAC, the successor to the "De-Baathification Commission" that worked since the fall of Saddam to purge former Baathists from government) invalidated the candidacies of 499 individuals (out of 6,500 candidates running) on many different slates. The JAC was headed by Ali al-Lami, but was heavily influenced by Ahmad Chalabi, who had headed the De-Baathification Commission. Both are Shiites, leading many to believe that the disqualifications represented an attempt to exclude prominent Sunnis. Appeals reinstated many of them, although about 300 had already been replaced by other candidates on their respective slates, including senior Iraqiyya figure Saleh al-Mutlaq. Al Lami was assassinated on May 26, 2011, presumably by Sunnis who viewed him as an architect of the perceived discrimination. Maliki later named the Minister for Human Rights to serve as JAC chairman concurrently. The JAC continues to vet candidates.

Election and Results

The final candidate list contained about 6,170 total candidates spanning 85 coalitions; the major coalitions are depicted in **Table 1**. Total turnout was about 62%, according to the IHEC. The final count was announced on March 26, 2010. As noted in **Table 3**, Iraqiyya won a narrow plurality of seats (two-seat margin over Maliki's State of Law slate). The Iraqi constitution (Article 73) mandates that the COR "bloc with the largest number" of members gets the first opportunity to form a government and Allawi demanded the first opportunity to form a government. However, on March 28, 2010, Iraq's Supreme Court ruled that a coalition that forms after the election could be deemed to meet that requirement, denying Allawi the first opportunity to form a government. The vote was to have been certified by April 22, 2010, but factional disputes delayed the certification. After appeals of some of the results, Iraq's Supreme Court certified the results on June 1, 2010, triggering the following timelines:

Post-Election Government

Part of the difficulty forming a government after the election was the perception that Iraqi politics is a "winner take all" proposition. In accordance with timelines established in the Constitution, the newly elected COR convened on June 15, 2010, but the session ended abruptly without electing a COR leadership team and subsequent constitutional deadlines to select a president, a prime minister, and a full government were not met. After months of deadlock, on October 1, 2010, Maliki received the backing of most of the 40 COR Sadrist deputies – appearing to guarantee Maliki would get a second term as prime minister . The Obama Administration backed a second Maliki term while demanding that Maliki form a government inclusive of Sunni leaders.

On November 10, 2010, with reported direct intervention by President Obama, the "Irbil Agreement" among major factions was finalized in which (1) Maliki and Talabani would remain in their offices for another term; (2) Iraqiyya would be extensively represented in government— one of its figures would become COR Speaker, another would be defense minister, and another (presumably Allawi himself) would chair an oversight body called the "National Council for Strategic Policies";[5] and (3) de-Baathification laws would be eased.

At the November 11, 2010, COR session to implement the agreement, Iraqiyya figure Usama al-Nujaifi (brother of Nineveh Governor Atheel Nujaifi) was elected COR speaker. Several days later, Talabani was reelected president and Talabani tapped Maliki as prime minister-designate, giving him until December 25, 2010, to achieve COR confirmation of a cabinet. That requirement as accomplished on December 21, 2010. Among major outcomes were the following:

- As for the State of Law list, Maliki remained prime minister, and retained for himself the Defense, Interior, and National Security (minister of state) posts pending permanent nominees for those positions. The faction took seven other cabinet posts, in addition to the post of first vice president (Khudayr al Khuzai of the Da'wa Party) and deputy prime minister for energy issues (Hussein Shahristani, previously the oil minister).
- For Iraqiyya, Saleh al-Mutlaq was appointed a deputy Prime Minister; Tariq al-Hashimi remained a vice president (second of three). The bloc also obtained nine ministerial posts, including Finance Minister Rafi al-Issawi (previously a deputy prime minister).
- The Iraqi National Alliance obtained 13 cabinet positions, parceled out among its various factions. The Sadrists got eight ministries, including Housing, Labor and Social Affairs, Ministry of Planning, and Tourism and Antiquities, as well as one of two deputy COR speakerships. An INA technocrat, Abd al Karim Luaibi, was appointed oil minister. A Fadilah party member, Bushra Saleh,

became minister of state without portfolio and the only woman in the cabinet at that time.

- The Kurdistan Alliance received major posts aside from Talabani. The third deputy prime minister is Kurdish/PUK figure Rows Shaways, who has served in various central and KRG positions since the fall of Saddam. Arif Tayfour is second deputy COR speaker. Alliance members had six other cabinet seats, including longtime Kurdish (KDP) stalwart Hoshyar Zebari remaining as foreign minister (a position he has held throughout the post-Saddam periods). Khairallah Hassan Babakir was named trade minister in February 13, 2011.

GRIEVANCES UNRESOLVED AS U.S. INVOLVEMENT CONCLUDES

The 2010 election in Iraq occurred near the end of the U.S. military presence in Iraq, which had begun to wind down in 2009 and was to conclude by the end of 2011. In addition to disputes over the power structure, numerous related issues were left unresolved, as discussed in the following sections.

Armed Sunni Groups

The power sharing arrangement reached among senior politicians did not produce dismantlement of the several Sunni armed groups that were operating in Iraq during and after the U.S. military exit from Iraq at the end of 2011. Such groups included Baath Party and Saddam Hussein supporters as well as hardline Islamists linked to Al Qaeda and Sunni tribal fighters. These armed groups comprised, broadly, the insurgency against U.S. forces in Iraq. The groups were relatively quiescent for the final two years of the U.S. presence in Iraq, but re-emerged to challenge stability and the Maliki government as Sunni unrest at Shiite pollitical domination has increased.

Al Qaeda in Iraq/Islamic State of Iraq and the Levant (ISIL)

Iraq's Al Qaeda affiliate constitutes the most violent component of the Sunni rebellion that has become a major threat to Iraqi stability in early 2014. Often cooperating with similarly named elements of the armed rebellion in neighboring Syria, the group currently operates in Iraq under the name of the

Islamic State of Iraq and the Levant (ISIL) or, alternately, Islamic State of Iraq and Syria, (ISIS).[6] The leader of AQ-I/ISIL is Abu Bakr Al Baghdadi, who is active both in Iraq and in Syria. U.S. officials estimated in November 2011 that there might be 800-1,000 AQ-I/ISIL members, of which some are involved in media or operations finance.[7] Although AQ-I/ISIL has focused on influencing the future of Iraq and, later, in Syria, the group has allegedly been responsible for some past attacks in Jordan. In October 2012, Jordanian authorities disrupted an alleged plot by AQ-I/ISIL to bomb multiple targets in Amman, Jordan, possibly including the U.S. Embassy there. However, the group does not appear to have close links to remaining senior Al Qaeda leaders believed mostly still in Pakistan or to Al Qaeda in the Arabian Peninsula (AQAP) in Yemen.

Attacks in Iraq attributed to AQ-I/ISIL escalated significantly after an assault on Sunni protesters in the town of Hawija incident on April 23, 2013, discussed below. According to some experts, AQ-I/ISIL is now able to carry out about 40 mass casualty attacks per month, much more than the 10 per month of 2010, and many AQ-I/ISIL attacks now span multiple cities.[8] In 2013, AQ-I/ISIL began asserting control of territory,[9] including operating some training camps in areas close to the Syria border. On July 21, 2013, when the group attacked prisons at Abu Ghraib and Taji; the Taji attack failed but the attacks on Abu Ghraib freed several hundred purported AQ-I/ISIL members. The attack on the heavily fortified Abu Ghraib—involving the use of suicide attackers and conventional tactics—shook confidence in the ISF. The head of the National Counterterrorism Center, Matt Olsen, told Congress on November 14, 2013, that AQ-I/ISIL is the strongest it has been since its peak in 2006.[10] During his visit to Washington, DC, during October 29-November 1, 2013, Maliki attributed virtually all the ongoing violence in Iraq to "terrorists" affiliated with AQ-I/ISIL, and downplayed the broader Sunnis resentment as a source of unrest.[11]

Naqshabandi Order (JRTN) and Ex-Saddam Military Commanders

Some groups that were prominent during the insurgency against U.S. forces remain allied with AQ-I/ISIL or active independently as part of the Sunni unrest. One such Sunni group, linked to ex-Baathists, is the Naqshabandi Order, known by its Arabic acronym "JRTN."[12] It is based primarily in Nineveh province and has been designated by the United States as a Foreign Terrorist Organization (FTO). Prior to the escalation of Sunni violence in 2013, the JRTN was responsible primarily for attacks on U.S. facilities in northern Iraq, which might have contributed to the State

Department decision in mid-2012 to close the Kirkuk consulate. The faction has supported Sunni demonstrators, and in February 2013 Sunnis linked to the JRTN circulated praise for the protests from the highest ranking Saddam regime figure still at large, Izzat Ibrahim al Duri. Other rebels are said to be linked to long-standing insurgent groups such as the 1920 Revolution Brigades or the Islamic Army of Iraq.

Generally aligned with the JRTN are ex-Saddam era military officers who were dismissed during the period of U.S. occupation and control in Iraq. Press reports in early 2014 said that ex-officers are the commanders of a new opposition structure called the "General Military Council for Iraqi Revolutionaries," which includes Sunni tribal fighters discussed below and other ex-insurgent figures.

Sons of Iraq Fighters

Another longstanding Sunni grievance has been the slow pace with which the Maliki government implemented its pledge to fully integrate the approximately 100,000 "Sons of Iraq" fighters. Also known as "Awakening" fighters, these are former insurgents who in 2006 began cooperating with U.S. forces against AQ-I/ISIL. Many of them are linked to the tribes of Anbar Province, but others are non-Al Qaeda Islamists that supported such Sunni Islamist organizations as the Muslim Scholars Association (MSA). The MSA is led by Harith al-Dari, who in 2006 fled U.S. counter-insurgency operations to live in Jordan. Harith al-Dari's son, Muthana, reportedly is active against the Maliki government currently.

During the later stages of the U.S. intervention in Iraq, the Iraqi government promised them integration into the Iraqi Security Forces (ISF) or government jobs. About 70,000 were integrated into the ISF or given civilian government jobs, while 30,000-40,000 continued to man checkpoints in Sunni areas and are paid about $300 per month by the government. In part to preserve the loyalty of the Sons of Iraq, in early 2013 the government increased their salaries by about 66% to $500 per month. The bulk of the Sons of Iraq fighters did not join the AQ-I/ISIL– led Sunni uprising in early 2014, but some did, according to many accounts.

The Sadr Faction and Shiite Militias

The 2006-2008 period of sectarian conflict was fueled in part by retaliatory attacks by Shiite militias, such as those that emanated from the faction of Shiite cleric Moqtada Al Sadr. The large Sadrist constituency, particularly among those who are on the lower economic echelons, has caused an inherent rivalry with Maliki and other Shiite leaders in Iraq. As noted, Sadr was part of an anti-Maliki Shiite coalition for the March 2010 elections, then supported Maliki for a second term, and later joined the unsuccessful effort to vote no-confidence against Maliki. Sadr says he opposes Maliki serving a third term subsequent to the April 30, 2014 elections. In February 2014, Sadr publicly announced his formal withdrawal from Iraqi politics, although Sadrist representatives remain in their posts and most experts assess that Sadr has continued influence over their activities. Sadrist candidates are competing in the April 30, 2014 elections.

Sadr's withdrawal from politics represents a departure from the high level of activity he has exhibited since he returned to Iraq, from his studies in Iran, in January 2011. After his return, he gave numerous speeches that, among other themes, insisted on full implementation of a planned U.S. withdrawal by the end of 2011. Sadr's position on the U.S. withdrawal appeared so firm that, in an April 9, 2011, statement, he threatened to reactivate his Mahdi Army militia if U.S. forces remained in Iraq beyond the December 31, 2011, deadline. In 2009, the Mahdi Army announced it would integrate into the political process as a charity and employment network called *Mumahidoon*, or "those who pave the way." Sadr's followers conducted a large march in Baghdad on May 26, 2011, demanding a full U.S. military exit. The threats were pivotal to the Iraqi decision not to retain U.S. troops in Iraq beyond 2011.

Sadrist Offshoots and Other Shiite Militias

Although Sadr formed what was the largest Shiite militia in post-Saddam Iraq, his efforts unleashed separate Shiite militant forces. They operate under names including Asa'ib Ahl al-Haq (AAH, League of the Family of the Righteous), Khata'ib Hezbollah (Hezbollah Battalions), and Promised Day Brigade. In June 2009, Khata'ib Hezbollah was named by the United States as a Foreign Terrorist Organization (FTO). On November 8, 2012, the Treasury Department designated several Khata'ib Hezbollah operatives, and their Iranian Revolutionary Guard—Qods Force mentors as terrorism supporting entities under Executive Order 13224.

The Shiite militias were part of an effort by Iran to ensure that the United States completely withdrew from Iraq. U.S. officials accused Shiite militias of causing an elevated level of U.S. troop deaths in June 2011 (14 killed, the highest in any month in over one year). During 2011, U.S. officials accused Iran of arming these militias with upgraded rocket-propelled munitions, such

Iraq: Politics, Governance, and Human Rights 19

as Improvised Rocket Assisted Munitions (IRAMs). U.S. officials reportedly requested that the Iraqi government prevail on Iran to stop aiding the militias, actions that temporarily quieted the Shiite attacks on U.S. forces in Iraq. Until the U.S. withdrawal in December 2011, some rocket attacks continued against the U.S. consulate in Basra, which has nearly 1,000 U.S. personnel (including contractors).

The U.S. exit in 2011 removed other militias' justification for armed activity and they moved into the political process. AAH's leaders returned from Iran and opened political offices, trying to recruit loyalists, and setting up social service programs. The group, reportedly supported by Iran, did not compete in the April 20, 2013, provincial elections but is competing as an informal Maliki ally in the 2014 national elections (Al Sadiqun, "the Friends," slate 218).[13] AAH's leader, Qais al-Khazali, took refuge in Iran in 2010 after three years in U.S. custody for his alleged role in a 2005 raid that killed five American soldiers.

Prior to 2013, experts had maintained that the Shiite militias were acting with restraint by not retaliating for Sunni attacks on Shiite citizens. However, as of mid-2013, this restraint apparently has weakened and some militias are conducting retaliatory attacks on Sunnis. In doing so, some experts see the militias as receiving the tacit cooperation of the Shiite-dominated ISF, particularly in Baghdad.[14] Iraqi Shiite militiamen are reportedly increasingly involved in Syria fighting and protecting Shiite shrines in support of the government of Bashar Al Assad.[15]

The Kurds and the Kurdistan Regional Government (KRG) [16]

Since the end of the U.S.-led war to liberate Kuwait in early 1991, the United States has played a role in protecting Iraq's Kurdish autonomy. Iraq's Kurds have tried to preserve this "special relationship" with the United States and use it to their advantage.

The Iraqi Kurds have long been divided between two main factions—the Patriotic Union of Kurdistan, PUK, and the Kurdistan Democratic Party, KDP. The two are abiding by a power sharing arrangement formalized in 2007, but they have a history of occasional and sometimes armed confrontation. The KRG has a President, Masoud Barzani, directly elected in July 2009, an elected Kurdistan National Assembly (KNA, sometimes called the Kurdistan Parliament of Iraq, or KPI), and an appointed Prime Minister. Since January 2012, the KRG Prime Minister has been Nechirvan Barzani (Masoud's nephew), who returned to that post after three years during in which the post was held by PUK senior figure Barham Salih. Masoud Barzani's son, Suroor, heads a KRG "national security council." Over the past five years, however, a new faction has emerged as a significant group in Kurdish politics—Gorran (Change), a PUK breakaway. The electoral success of Gorran, coupled with the continued infirmity of Iraqi President Jalal Talabani (head of the PUK), has shifted political strength within the KRG to the KDP and away from the PUK.

The Iraqi Kurds also—as permitted in the Iraqi constitution—field their own force of *peshmerga* (Kurdish militiamen) numbering perhaps 75,000 fighters. They are generally lightly armed. Kurdish leaders continue to criticize Maliki for paying out of the national budget only about half of the total peshmerga force (those who are under the control of the KRG's Ministry of Peshmerga Affairs). However, about half are not incorporated into this structure and are funded out of the KRG budget. The KRG is in the process of reforming the *peshmerga* into a smaller but more professional and well trained force.

Since 2001, U.S. immigration officials have placed the KDP and PUK in a "Tier Three" category that makes it difficult for members of the parties to obtain visas to enter the United States. The categorization is a determination that the two parties are "groups of concern" – meaning some of their members have committed acts of political violence. The designation was based on the fact that the Kurdish parties, particularly their *peshmerga*, had used violence to try to overthrow the government of Saddam Hussein. The designation was made before the United States militarily overthrew Saddam in 2003, and has not been revoked.

The characterization seems to many in Congress and the Administration to be inconsistent with the close political relations between the United States and the KDP and PUK. KRG President Barzani has said he will not visit the United States until the designation is removed. Two bills, H.R. 4474 and S. 2255 would legislatively remove the PUK and KDP from Tier 3 categorization. On April 14, 2014, State Dept. spokeswoman Jen Psaki said the Administration supports the legislation.

KRG-Baghdad Relations

Senior Iraq's Kurdish leaders have long said they do not seek outright independence or affiliation with Kurds in neighboring countries, but rather to secure and expand the autonomy they have achieved in Iraq. However, the issues dividing the KRG and Baghdad have expanded to the point where some

KRG President Barzani has begun to assert that the KRG might seek independence, but without use of violence against the central government. Following a visit to Washington, DC, in April 2012 and since, Barzani has threatened to hold a vote on Kurdish independence unless Maliki holds to his pledges of power-sharing and resolves major issues with the KRG.[17] As noted, Kurds in the COR joined the failed 2012 effort to vote no confidence against Maliki. The animosity continued in 2013, but the Kurdish leadership and Maliki have continued to engage and exchange views and visits. Maliki made his first visit to Irbil in two years on June 10, 2013 and Barzani visited Bagdhad on July 7, 2013, his first since late 2010. The two sides subsequently established seven joint committees to try to resolve the major disputes between them.[18] Some reports suggest that the Kurdish leaders might accept Maliki's selection to a third term as Prime Minister.

As do political tensions, disputes between the forces of the two political entities sometimes come close to major conflict. In November 2012, a commercial dispute between an Arab and Kurd in Tuz Khurmatu, a town in Salahuddin Province straddling the Baghdad-KRG territorial border, caused a clash and a buildup of ISF and Kurdish troops facing off. Several weeks of U.S. and intra-Iraq mediation resulted in a tentative agreement on December 6, 2012, for both sides to pull back their forces and for local ethnic groups to form units to replace ISF and *peshmerga* units along the Baghdad-KRG frontier. The agreement was only partially implemented. In May 2013, peshmerga forces advanced their positions in Kirkuk province, taking advantage of the ISF drawdown there as the ISF dealt with Sunni violence elsewhere in Iraq.

The continued clashes and frontier tensions could be attributed, in part, to the end of the "combined security mechanism" (CSM) set up by the United States when its troops were in Iraq. The CSM began in January 2010, consisting of joint (ISF-U.S-Kurdish) patrols, maintenance of 22 checkpoints, and U.S. training of participating ISF and *peshmerga* forces. The mechanism was administered through provincial level Combined Coordination Centers, and disagreements were referred to a Senior Working Group and a High Level Ministerial Committee.[19]

Kirkuk Dispute

The KRG-Baghdad clashes have been spurred in part by the lack of any progress in recent years in resolving the various territorial disputes between the Kurds and Iraq's Arabs. The most emotional of these is the Kurdish insistence that Tamim Province (which includes oil-rich Kirkuk) is "Kurdish land" and must be formally affiliated to the KRG. There was to be a census and referendum on the affiliation of the province by December 31, 2007, under Article 140 of the Constitution, but the Kurds have agreed to repeated delays in order to avoid jeopardizing overall progress in Iraq. Nor has the national census that is pivotal to any such referendum been conducted; it was scheduled for October 24, 2010, but then repeatedly postponed by the broader political crisis and differences over how to account for movements of populations into or out of the Kurdish-controlled provinces.

On the other hand, some KRG-Baghdad disputes have moved forward. The Property Claims Commission that is adjudicating claims from the Saddam regime's forced resettlement of Arabs into the KRG region is functioning. Of the 178,000 claims received, nearly 26,000 were approved and 90,000 rejected or ruled invalid by the end of 2011, according to the State Department. Since 2003, more than 28,000 Iraqi Arabs settled in the KRG area by Saddam have relocated from Kirkuk back to their original provinces.

KRG Oil Exports

The KRG and Baghdad are still at odds over the Kurds' insistence that it export oil that is discovered and extracted in the KRG region. Baghdad reportedly fears that Kurdish oil exports can potentially enable the Kurds to set up an economically viable independent state and has called the KRG's separate energy development deals with international firms "illegal." Baghdad has supported KRG oil exports through the national oil export pipeline grid in which revenues from the KRG exports go into central government accounts, proceeds (17% agreed proportion) go to the KRG, and Baghdad pays the international oil companies working in the KRG.

KRG oil exports through the national grid have been repeatedly suspended over central government withholding of payments to the international energy firms. In September 2012, the KRG and Baghdad agreed that Baghdad would pay arrears due the international firms. However, that pact held only until late December 2012. The 2013 budget adopted by the COR on March 7, 2013, allocated only $650 million to the companies exporting KRG oil; the Kurds had sought the full $3.5 billion owed international firms for that purpose. The Kurds boycotted a March 17, 2014 COR vote on the first reading of the 2014-15 national budget which again fails to compensate international firms the $5 billion they are owed (as of March 2014) for Kurdish oil and demands that the KRG export at least 400,000 barrels per day of oil using Iraqi national export routes and marketing institutions. According to the budget bill, any shortfall below that export total would be deducted from the KRG's 17% share of the oil revenue received. The budget has not been adopted to date because of this dispute. And, to maintain leverage in the dispute, since January 2014, the Iraqi government has suspended all but a small fraction of its payments of about $1 billion per month to the KRG on the grounds that the KRG is not contributing oil revenue to the national coffers.

In the absence of agreement between the KRG and Baghdad, the KRG has exported some oil through a newly constructed pipeline to Turkey (that the Kurds assert bypasses the Iraqi national grid, even though it intersects in Turkey with the Iraq-Turkey pipeline controlled by Baghdad) capable of carrying 300,000 barrels per day of oil. However, the oil (1.5 million barrels) has thus far been stored pending resolution of the dispute over whether the KRG or Baghdad have the right to market the oil and collect the revenue.[20] The KRG trucks an additional 60,000 barrels per day to Turkey. KRG fields currently have the potential to export 500,000 barrels per day and it is expected to be able to increase exports to 1 million barrels per day by 2019,[21] if export routes are available. The Obama Administration has generally sided with Baghdad on the dispute, asserting that major international energy projects involving Iraq should be negotiated and implemented through a unified central government in Baghdad.

Related to the disputes over KRG oil exports is a broader disagreement over foreign firm involvement in the KRG energy sector. The central government has sought to deny energy deals with the central government to companies that sign development deals with the KRG. This dispute has affected such firms as Exxon-Mobil and Total SA of France.

KRG Elections and Intra-Kurdish Divisions

Provincial elections in the KRG-controlled provinces were not held during the nationwide January 2009 provincial elections or during the March 7, 2010, COR vote. In April 2013, the KRG announced that elections would be held in 2013 for provincial councils in the three KRG provinces, for the KNA, and for the KRG presidency. However, on July 1, 2013, the KNA voted, after substantial debate, to extend Barzani's term two years, until August 19, 2015. The State Department said on July 2, 2013, that it is confident that the KNA elected in September would finalize a KRG constitution and set presidential elections possibly earlier than that term expiration. Subsequently, the IHEC, which runs elections even in the KRG area, persuaded the KRG it could not also hold provincial elections on the same day as the KNA elections. The KNA elections were confirmed for September 21, 2013, and the KRG provincial elections were scheduled for November 21, 2013. On October 8,

2013, the IHEC announced that the provincial elections in the KRG region would be held concurrent with the Iraq-wide parliamentary elections on April 30, 2014.

September 21, 2013, KNA Elections. The KNA elections went forward on September 21, 2013 as planned, and further complicated the political landscape in the KRG. About 1,130 candidates registered to run for the 111 available seats, 11 of which are reserved for minority communities that live in the north, such as Yazidis, Shabaks, Assyrians, and others. The 2013 KNA elections continued a trend begun in the previous KNA elections of March 2010 in which Gorran emerged as a major player. Headed by Neshirvan Mustafa, Gorran won an unexpectedly high 25 KNA seats in March 2010 and won 24 seats in the September 21, 2013, KNA election. The 2013 result was particularly significant because in the 2013 election, the KDP and the PUK ran separately, not combined as the Kurdistan Alliance. In the 2013 vote, Gorran's 24 seats placed it second to the KDP's 38 (up from 30 in 2010). The PUK was humbled by coming in third with only 18 seats, down from 29 in the 2010 election. The results have elevated Gorran's political strength, a contributing factor to the Kurds' inability to reorganize the KRG government to date. Kurdish officials say they hope to complete the governmental reorganization before the April 30. 2014 Iraqi national election.

Many experts on the Kurdish region attribute the PUK's showing in the 2013 KNA elections to the infirmity of Iraq's President and PUK leader Jalal Talabani and the attendant turmoil in the PUK leadership. Talabani remains in Germany to recuperate from his stroke, although he has not stepped down as Iraq's President. Barham Salih, mentioned above, is said to be pressing to replace Talabani as president after the April 30, 2014 national elections, in part because the Kurds do not want the Kurds to lose control of the position of president to a Sunni Arab. Another PUK stalwart, Kosrat Rasoul, who serves as KRG Vice President, is said to be seeking support to succeed Talabani as PUK leader. Talabani's son, Qubad, who headed the KRG representative office in Washington, DC, until returning to the KRG in July 2012, has become more involved in Kurdish and PUK politics as his father's health fades. Talabani's wife, Hero Ibrahim Ahmad Talabani, is also a major figure in PUK politics and is said to be an opponent of Kosrat Rasoul.

POST-U.S. WITHDRAWAL POLITICAL UNRAVELING

With the grievances discussed above unresolved, armed factions still able and willing to use violence to achieve their objectives, and U.S. forces not present in large numbers to suppress violence, the 2010 power-sharing arrangement unraveled. Throughout 2011, Maliki's opponents became increasingly vocal in accusing him of concentrating power in his and his faction's hands – in particular his appointment of allies as "acting" ministers of three key security ministries— Defense, Interior, and National Security (intelligence) while retaining those portfolios for himself.[22] Through his Office of the Commander-in-Chief, Maliki directly commands the 10,000 person Counter-Terrorism Service, of which about 4,100 are Iraqi Special Operations Forces (ISOF). These forces are tasked with countering militant groups, although Maliki's critics assert that he uses them to intimidate his senior Sunni critics and Iraq's Sunnis more broadly.

Critics assert that Maliki also put under his executive control several supposedly independent bodies. In late 2010, he successfully requested that Iraq's Supreme Court rule that the Independent Higher Election Commission (IHEC) that runs Iraq's elections and the Commission of Integrity, the key anti-corruption body be supervised by the cabinet.[23] In March 2012, Maliki also asserted governmental control over the Central Bank.

On December 19, 2011, the day after the final U.S. withdrawal (December 18, 2011)—and one week after Maliki met with President Obama in Washington, DC, on December 12, 2011—the government announced an arrest warrant against Vice President Tariq al-Hashimi, a major Sunni Iraqiyya figure, for allegedly ordering his security staff to commit acts of assassination. Hashimi fled to the KRG region and refused to return to face trial in Baghdad unless his conditions for a fair trial there were met. A trial in absentia in Baghdad convicted him and sentenced him to death on September 9, 2012, for the alleged killing of two Iraqis. Hashimi remains in Turkey, where he eventually fled.

The arrest cast doubt on President Obama's assertion, marking the U.S. withdrawal, that Iraq is now "sovereign, stable, and self-reliant." U.S. officials immediately attempted to contain the crisis by intervening with the various political factions. The effort produced some results when Maliki released some Baathists prisoners and agreed to legal amendments to give provinces more budgetary autonomy and the right of consent when national security forces are deployed.[24] (These concessions were included in a revised provincial powers law adopted by the COR in June 2013, as discussed above.) The concessions prompted Iraqiyya COR deputies and ministers to resume their duties by early February 2012.

Failed Effort to Oust Maliki Politically in 2012. In March 2012, the factions tentatively agreed to hold a "national conference," to be chaired by President Talabani, respected as an even-handed mediator, to try to reach a durable political solution. However, late that month KRG President Barzani accused Maliki of a "power grab" and the conference was not held. Maliki critics Allawi, COR speaker Osama Nujaifi, and Moqtada Al Sadr met in April 2012 in the KRG region and subsequently collected signatures from 176 COR deputies to request a no-confidence vote against Maliki's government. Under Article 61 of the constitution, signatures of 20% of the 325 COR deputies (65 signatures) are needed to trigger a vote, but President Talabani (who is required to present a valid request to the COR to hold the vote) stated on June 10, 2012 that there were an insufficient number of valid signatures remaining to proceed with that vote.[25] Maliki apparently convinced many Sadrists COR deputies to remove their signatures. Maliki also reinstated deputy Prime Minister Saleh al-Mutlaq as part of an effort to reach out to Sunni leaders.

Political Crisis Reopens Broader Sectarian Rift in 2013

Political disputes flared again after the widely respected President Talabani suffered a stroke on December 18, 2012 and was flown out of Iraq for treatment. On December 20, 2012, Maliki moved against another perceived Sunni adversary, Finance Minister Rafi al-Issawi, by arresting 10 of his bodyguards. He resigned as Finance Minister and took refuge in Anbar province with Sunni tribal leaders. The actions against Issawi sparked anti-Maliki demonstrations in the Sunni cities of Anbar, Salahuddin, and Nineveh provinces, as well as in Sunni districts of Baghdad. (Talabani has remained in Germany since for rehabilitation, and second Vice President Khudayr Khuzai has served as acting President.)

As demonstrations continued, what had been primarily disputes among elites was transformed into substantial public unrest. The thrust of the Sunni complaints was based on perceived discrimination by the Shiite-dominated Maliki government. Some Sunni demonstrators were reacting not only to the moves against senior Sunni leaders, but also to the fact that the overwhelming majority of prisoners in Iraq's jails are Sunnis, according to Human Rights Watch researchers. Sunni demonstrators demanded the release of prisoners, particularly women; a repeal of "Article 4" anti-terrorism laws under which many Sunnis are incarcerated; reform or end to the de-Baathification laws that has been used against Sunnis; and improved government services.[26]

During January-March 2013, the use of small amounts of force against demonstrators caused the unrest to worsen. On January 25, 2013, the ISF killed nine protesters on a day when oppositionists killed two ISF police officers. Sunni demonstrators protested every Friday during that period, and began to set up encampments in some cities. Some observers maintained that the protest movement was emboldened by the Sunni-led rebellion in neighboring Syria.

The Sunni unrest, coupled with the U.S. departure, provided "political space" for long-standing violent Sunni elements to revive. Violent Sunni elements—weakened but never totally eliminated by the United States during 2003-2011—reactivated to try to reinforce peaceful Sunni protesters; undermine confidence in the ISF; expel Shiite members of the ISF from Sunni areas; and reignite the sectarian war that prevailed during 2006-2008. All of these motivations, in the apparent view of the militants, could have the effect of destabilizing Maliki and his Shiite-led rule. To try to accomplish these goals, Sunni militant groups have attacked pilgrims to the various Shiite shrines and holy sites in Iraq; Shiite neighborhoods and businesses; ISF personnel; government installations; and some Sunnis who are cooperating with the government.

The unrest prompted some further rifts and leadership responses. The COR passed a law limiting Maliki to two terms, although Iraq's Supreme Court struck that law down in mid-2013. In March 2013, Kurdish ministers suspended their participation in the central government. Maliki tried to mollify the Sunni leaders and protesters by forming a committee, headed by Deputy Prime Minister Shahristani, to examine protester grievances and suggest reforms and by releasing some imprisoned Sunnis.

Escalation of Violence Since April 2013 Hawijah Incident

On April 23, 2013, three days after the first group of provinces voted in provincial elections, the ISF stormed a Sunni protest camp in the town of Hawijah, near the mostly Kurdish city of Kirkuk. About 40 civilians and three ISF personnel were killed in the battle that ensued. In the following days, many Sunni demonstrators and tribal leaders took up arms and called on followers to arm themselves. Sunni gunmen took over government buildings in the town of Suleiman Pak for a few days. At the political level, Iraqiyya pulled out of the COR entirely, and three Sunni ministers resigned. In a speech to the nation on April 24, 2013, Maliki urged dialogue but also stated that the ISF "must impose security in Iraq."

U.S. officials reportedly pressed Maliki not to use the military to suppress Sunni protests, arguing that such a strategy has led to all-out civil war in neighboring Syria, and also worked with Sunni tribal leaders to appeal for calm. On April 30, 2013, following meetings with central government members, Kurdish leaders agreed to return Kurdish ministers to their positions in Baghdad.

Even as the major factions tried to restore mutual trust, Sunni Arab attacks on government forces, Shiite gathering places, and even against other Sunnis cooperating with the government escalated. Many of these attacks—particularly the simultaneous multiple-target attacks—were carried out by AQ-I/ISIL. According to the U.N. Assistance Mission-Iraq (UNAMI), about 9,000 Iraqis were killed in 2013, of whom all but about 1,000 were civilians, and the remainder were members of the ISF. This was more than double the death toll for all of 2010, and the highest total since the height of sectarian conflict in 2006-2007, although still about 60% below those levels.

Tentative signs emerged in mid-2013 that Shiite armed groups might be reactivating to retaliate against the Sunni-led attacks on the Shiite community. The ISF, which is largely Shiite and perceived by Sunnis as aligned with the Shiite community, has put significant security measures into effect in Baghdad. These included the establishment of numerous checkpoints and restricting movements of cars in order to be able to check the contents of each one. Sunnis complain that these measures are discriminatory and essentially confine them to enclaves. The abduction and killing of 18 Sunnis in Baghdad on November 29, 2013 was allegedly carried out by Shiite militiamen.[27]

Maliki undertook gestures toward the Sunnis, although the actions did not end the unrest. In June 2013 the COR amended the 2008 provincial powers law (No. 21, see above) to give the provinces substantially more authority relative to the central government, including some control over security forces (Article 31-10). The revisions also specify a share of revenue to be given to the provinces and mandate that within two years, control of the province-based operations of central government ministries be transferred to the provincial governments.[28] In July 2013, the cabinet approved a package of reforms easing the de-Baathification laws to allow many former Baathists to hold government positions—a key demand of the Sunni protesters. During his visit to Washington, D.C. during October 2013, Maliki denied he has sought to marginalize Sunni leaders and asserted that all his actions were taken under his authority in the Iraqi constitution.[29]

Iraq: Politics, Governance, and Human Rights

April 2013 Provincial Elections Occur Amid the Tensions

The escalating violence affected, but did not derail, 2013 provincial elections. The mandate of the nine-member IHEC, which runs the election, expired at the end of April 2012, and the COR confirmed a new panel in September 2012. On October 30, 2012, the IHEC set an April 20, 2013, election date, while deciding that provincial elections would not be held in the three KRG-controlled provinces or in the province of Kirkuk. The COR's law to govern the election for the 447 provincial council seats (including those in Anbar and Nineveh that voted on June 20, 2013) passed in December 2012, providing for an open list vote. A total of 50 coalitions registered, including 261 political entities as part of those coalitions or running separately. About 8,150 individual candidates registered, of which 200 were later barred by the JAC for alleged Baathist ties. Because of the escalating violence, the government postponed the elections in two Sunni provinces, Anbar and Nineveh, until June 20, 2013. The KRG set September 21, 2013, to vote for Kurdistan National Assembly elections, but not a vote for any other posts, as discussed below.

The results appeared to demonstrate that most Iraqis want to rebuild political power-sharing. With the April 20, 2013, vote being held mostly in Shiite areas, the election was largely a test of Maliki's popularity. Maliki's State of Law coalition remained relatively intact, consisting mostly of Shiite parties, including Fadilah (Virtue) and the ISCI-offshoot the Badr Organization. ISCI registered its own "Citizen Coalition,") and Sadr registered a separate "Coalition of Liberals." Among the mostly Sunni groupings, Allawi's Iraqiyya and 18 smaller entities ran as the "Iraqi National United Coalition." A separate "United Coalition" consisted of supporters of the Nujaifis (COR speaker and Nineveh governor), Vice President Tariq al-Hashimi, and Rafi al-Issawi. A third Sunni coalition was loyal to Saleh al-Mutlaq. The two main Kurdish parties ran under the Co-Existence and Fraternity Alliance.

Turnout on April 20, 2013, was estimated at about 50% of registered voters. Election day violence was minimal, although 16 Sunni candidates were assassinated prior to the election. According to results finalized on May 19, 2013, Maliki's State of Law won a total of about 112 seats—about 22%, down from the 29% it won in 2009, but a plurality in 7 of the 12 provinces that voted. The loss of some of its seats cost Maliki's list control of the key provincial councils of Baghdad and Basra. ISCI's Citizen Coalition won back some of the losses it suffered in the 2009 elections, winning about 75 seats. Sadr's slate won 59 seats, including a plurality in Maysan province. Among

Sunnis, the United Coalition bested the Iraqiyya-led coalition, an outcome most relevant in the two majority Sunni provinces that voted that day—Diyala and Salahuddin.

The June 20, 2013, election in Anbar and Nineveh was primarily a contest among the Sunni blocs. In heavily Sunni Anbar, the Nujaifi bloc won a slight plurality, but newly emerging leaders there selected as governor Ahmad Khalaf al-Dulaimi, who works amicably with the Maliki government. In Nineveh, where the Nujaifis previously held an outright majority of provincial council seats (19 or 37), Kurds won 11 out of the province's 39 seats. The Nujaifi grouping came in second with eight seats, but Atheel Nujaifi was selected to another term as governor. The results suggested to some experts that many Sunnis want to avoid a return to sectarian conflict.[30]

Major Uprising Flares in Late 2013

After the provincial elections, unrest in Sunni areas continued but did not escalate sharply until the end of 2013. A major upsurge in Sunni Arab unrest began on December 26, 2013 when, following an ISIL attack that killed 17 ISF officers, Maliki sought the arrest of Sunni parliamentarian Ahmad al-Alwani on charges of inciting anti-government activity. The arrest prompted a gun battle with security forces that killed Alwani's brother and several of his bodyguards. Maliki subsequently ordered security forces to close down a protest tent camp in Ramadi, the capital of Anbar Province. That action prompted significant rebellion in both Ramadi and Fallujah by ISIL, later spreading, to lesser degrees, to other Sunni cities in and outside Anbar. Both Ramadi and Fallujah were major objectives of U.S. counterinsurgency efforts during the Iraq war. ISIL fighters, joined by some Sunni protesters, defectors from the Iraq Security Forces (ISF), and some Sons of Iraq and other tribal fighters, took over major parts of both Ramadi and Fallujah and burned police stations in these cities, freed prisoners, and captured or destroyed many ISF vehicles. However, most Sons of Iraq fighters appear to have obeyed the urgings of many tribal leaders' urgings to back the government and help suppress the ISIL-led insurrection.

Partly at the urging of U.S. officials, Maliki opted not to order an ISF assault but to instead provide weapons and funding to Sunni tribal leaders and Sons of Iraq fighters who stood with the government so that they could expel the ISIL fighters themselves. Maliki also signaled compromise by ordering the arrest of a Shiite hardliner, "Mukhtar Army" leader Wahtiq al-Batat and ordered the ISF to cease attacking homes—a gesture to the Sunni population. By the end of the first week of January 2014, the government had regained most of Ramadi, but Fallujah remained in insurgent hands. In early April 2014, ISIL-led insurgents also established a presence in Abu Ghraib, which is only ten miles from Baghdad. Iraq closed the prison because of the security threat and transferred the prisoners to other prisons around Iraq. In mid-April 2014, the government urged Fallujah citizens to leave the city in advance of government air strikes on insurgent positions, although the strikes did not dislodge the rebels. Some ISF officers have told journalists the ISF effort to assist in the recapture of Fallujah and small locations under opposition control has been disorganized and ineffective.[31] Insurgents also have continued to attack Shiite civilian and ISF and government targets in Baghdad and other several other cities. As a result of the insurrection, an estimate 140,000 Iraqis have left Anbar Province, relocating mostly to Baghdad according to press accounts.

U.S. Response to the Insurrection. The major escalation of violence in Iraq in early 2014 insurrection has caused the Obama Administration to take a more active role in Iraq. On January 5, 2014, Secretary of State John Kerry said the United States would provide the Iraqi government help to deal with the crisis, but he directly ruled out the possibility of U.S. reintroduction of ground troops to Iraq.[32] As outlined below, including in House Foreign Affairs Committee testimony of February 5, 2014 by Deputy Assistant Secretary of State Brett McGurk, the United States is encouraging Maliki to take a "holistic" strategy of combatting ISIL and also accommodating his Sunni opponents. The United States has:

- *Delivered and sold additional weaponry.* In late December 2013, the Defense Department sent 75 HELLFIRE missiles as well as unarmed surveillance drones to the ISF for use against ISIS camps. However, the missiles were for use by Iraq's propeller-driven aircraft, because the Administration turned down an Iraqi request to transfer armed drones for that same purpose. On January 23, the Defense Security Cooperation Agency (DSCA) notified Congress of a 2014, proposed sale to Iraq of an additional 500 HELLFIRES and associated training and equipment, at an estimated cost of $82 million. 100 of the missiles were delivered in late March 2014, according to press reports. The Administration also obtained the concurrence of Congress to release for sale and lease 30 "Apache" attack helicopters to Iraq. Some in Congress had earlier held up provision of these aircraft out of concerns that the Iraqi government would use the attack helicopters against non-violent opponents. The United States also is providing unarmed surveillance drones, as discussed below.

- *Additional Training.* The Department of Defense has increased bilateral and regional training opportunities for Iraqi counterterrorism (CT) units; Iraq and Jordan are discussing advanced training for Iraqi forces in Jordan.[33] The training would presumably help burnish ISF counter-insurgency skills that, according to several experts, have lapsed since the departure of U.S. troops in 2011. By all accounts, other than weapons and equipment deliveries, there has been no direct U.S. military involvement in or assistance to the ISF responses in Anbar.

- *Efforts at Accommodation.* U.S. officials, including Vice President Biden, who is reported to have played a major role in the Administration's Iraq policy to date, reportedly have been in contact with Maliki and his Sunni and Kurdish opponents to encourage dialogue and accommodation. As noted above, in an apparent gesture to the Sunnis community and minority communities in the north, on January 21, 2014 the Iraqi government announced a plan to create three new provinces, including one centered on the restive city of Fallujah. Provinces are able to obtain and control financial resources more readily than subordinate localities.

April 30, 2014, COR Elections

The escalating violence has the potential to disrupt the COR elections to be held on April 30, 2014, in particular by preventing any voting in insurgent-held areas. Because a new government is chosen by the elected parliament, postponing the election in restive areas only is not a realistic option. There are likely to be some international election observers present, but likely few or none in the restive cities of Anbar, and it is doubtful that there will be any voting in Fallujah.

An election law to regulate the election was the subject of debate primarily between the Kurds and Maliki's allies, delaying passage of the election law until November 4, 2013—slightly beyond the IHEC-imposed deadline of October 31. The Kurds had sought to have the 2005 election system used, in which all of Iraq is considered one district. Maliki and other Shiites prevailed in their preference to use the system employed in the 2010 elections, in which voters cast votes in specific districts. The election law expanded the number of seats of the new COR to 328, an increase of three seats (all three are from the KRG region).

A total of 39 coalitions, comprising 275 political entities (parties), some of which will run separately, have registered. Maliki's State of Law bloc remains relatively intact and many rival blocs have fractured since the 2010 election – making his return to the Prime Ministership highly likely. Shiite blocs are likely, as they did in 2010, to unify after the election to ensure there is a Shiite Prime Minister—and Maliki appears to be the strongest among them. The Iraqiyya bloc, for example, which won more seats than did State of Law in 2010, has fragmented into components led by various Sunni and other leaders, as shown in the table below. The major Kurdish factions appear to be a united coalition, as has been the case previously, although they might compete separately in some areas. And, the Kurdish party Gorran is more of a force than it has been previously, and it is running separately—potentially reducing Kurdish leverage in post-election Iraqi government formation.

Because President Talabani remains outside Iraq, it is virtually certain that a different president will be selected after the election. However, it is possible that the Sunnis might argue that a Sunni become President; if that argument is made and prevails, the Sunnis would presumably yield the COR speakership to a Kurdish official. The major coalitions are in the table below.

The April 30, 2014 elections will also include elections for 89 total seats on the provincial councils in the three KRG provinces. The campaign period nationwide began on April 1.

GOVERNANCE, ECONOMIC RESOURCES, AND HUMAN RIGHTS ISSUES

The continuing political crises discussed above have dashed most hopes that Iraq will become a fully functioning democracy with well-established institutions and rule of law. On the other hand, some experts assert that most Iraqis remain committed to the success of the existing governing structure and that all the outstanding disputes are soluble and that the success of Iraq's energy sector is mitigating these adverse factors.

Energy Sector and Economic Development

Adopting national oil laws has been considered key to developing and establishing rule of law and transparency in a key sector. Substantial progress appeared near in August 2011 when both the COR and the cabinet drafted the oil laws long in the works to rationalize the energy sector and clarify the rules for foreign investors. However, there were differences in their individual versions: the version drafted by the Oil and Natural Resources Committee was presented to the full COR on August 17, 2011. The cabinet adopted its separate version on August 28, 2011—a version that the KRG opposed as favoring too much "centralization" (i.e., Baghdad control) in the energy sector. The September 2012 KRG-Baghdad agreement on KRG oil exports included a provision to set up a six-member committee to review the different versions of the oil laws under consideration and decide which version to submit to the COR for formal consideration. However, no definitive movement on this issue has been announced since.

Table 2. Major Coalitions in April 30, 2014 COR Elections

Coalition	Leaders and Components
State of Law (Slate No. 277)	Maliki and his Da'wa Party; deputy P.M. Shahristani (both running in Baghdad); Badr Organization (ISCI offshoot)
Muwatin (Citizens Coalition) (273)	ISCI list. Includes former Interior Minister Bayan Jabr Solagh; Ahmad Chalabi; many Basra politicians
Al Ahrar (Liberals) (214)	Sadrists. Allied with ISCI in 2010 but separate in 2014.
Wataniya (Nationalists) (239)	Iyad al-Allawi (running in Baghdad), Includes Allawi followers from former Iraqiyya bloc
Mutahiddun (United Ones) (259)	COR Speaker Nujaifi (running in Nineveh). No candidates in Shiite-dominated provinces. Was part of Allawi Iraqiyya bloc in 2010.
Arabiyya (Arabs) (255)	deputy P.M. Saleh al-Mutlaq (running in Baghdad) Also limited to mostly Sunni provinces. Was part of Iraqiyya bloc in 2010.
Kurdistan Alliance	KDP and PUK, but running separately in some constituencies.
Fadilah (219)	Shiite faction, was allied with ISCI in 2010 election but running separately in 2014.
Da'wa (Jaafari) (205)	Da'wa faction of former P.M. Ibrahim al-Jafari (who is running in Karbala). Was allied with ISCI in 2010.

Source: Reidar Vissar, "Iraq and Gulf Analysis.

The continuing deadlock on oil laws has not, however, prevented growth in the crucial energy sector, which provides 90% of Iraq's budget. Iraq possesses a proven 143 billion barrels of oil. After long remaining below the levels achieved prior to the ouster of Saddam Hussein, Iraq's oil exports recovered to Saddam-era levels of about 2.1 million barrels per day by March 2012. Production reached the milestone 3 million barrels per day mark in February 2012, which Iraqi leaders trumpeted as a key milestone in Iraq's recovery, and expanded further to about 3.6 million barrels per day as of early April 2014. The growth in Iraq's exports has contributed to keeping the global oil market well supplied as the oil customers of neighboring Iran have cut back Iranian oil purchases in cooperation with U.S. sanctions on Iran.

Iraqi leaders say they want to increase production to over 10 million barrels per day by 2017. The International Energy Agency estimates more modest but still significant gains: it sees Iraq reaching 6 mbd of production by 2020 if it attracts $25 billion in investment per year, and potentially 8 mbd by 2035.

What is helping the Iraqi production is the involvement of foreign firms, including BP, Exxon-Mobil, Occidental, and Chinese firms. China now buys about half of Iraq's oil exports. Chinese firms such as China National Petroleum Corp. (CNPC) are major investors in several Iraqi fields. U.S. firms assisted Iraq's export capacity by developing single-point mooring oil loading terminals to compensate for deterioration in Iraq's existing oil export infrastructure in Basra and Umm Qasr. Press reports in November 2013 say that Royal Dutch Shell and the Iraqi government are close to an $11 billion deal for the firm to build a petrochemical production facilitiy in southern Iraq. This would follow a $17 billion 2012 deal between the company and Iraq to produce natural gas that were previously flared in Iraq's southern oil fields.

Oil Resources Fuels Growth

The growth of oil exports appears to be fueling a rapid expansion of the economy. Iraqi officials estimated that growth was about 9% for 2013. Press reports have noted the development of several upscale malls and other consequences of positive economic progress. The more stable areas of Iraq, such as the Shiite south, are said to be experiencing an economic boom as they accommodate increasing numbers of Shiite pilgrims to Najaf and Karbala. Iraqi officials said in mid-February 2013 that the country now has about $105 billion in foreign exchange reserves. GDP reached about $150 billion by the end of 2013. On September 18, 2013, Iraq launched a $357 billion five-year National Development Plan, with projects across many different sectors. As discussed above, Iraq's cabinet and COR are debating a $150 billion budget for 2014 but it has not been adopted because of disputes with the KRG over KRG oil export revenue issues.

General Human Rights Issues

The State Department human rights report for 2013, released February 27, 2014, largely repeated the previous years' criticisms of Iraq's human rights record. The report for 2013 states that a "culture of impunity" largely protected members of the security services and others in government from accountability or punishment for abuses.[34] The State Department report cited a wide range of human rights problems committed by Iraqi government security and law enforcement personnel—as well as by KRG security institutions—including unlawful killings; torture and other cruel punishments; poor conditions in prison facilities; denial of fair public trials; arbitrary arrest; arbitrary interference with privacy and home; limits on freedoms of speech, assembly, and association due to sectarianism and extremist threats; lack of protection of stateless persons; wide scale governmental corruption; human trafficking; and limited exercise of labor rights. Many of these same abuses and deficiencies are alleged in reports by outside groups such as Human Rights Watch.

On the other hand, U.S. officials assert that civil society organizations are expanding in size and authority to perform formal and informal oversight of human rights in Iraq. During a visit to Iraq on June 28-30, 2013, Deputy Secretary of State William Burns awarded the 2012 "Human Rights Defender Award" to an Iraqi human rights organization, the Hammurabi Human Rights Organization.

Trafficking in Persons

The State Department's Trafficking in Persons report for 2013, released on June 19, 2013, places Iraq in "Tier 2." That was an upgrade from the Tier 2 Watch List rating for Iraq for four previous years. The upgrade was a product of the U.S. assessment that Iraq is making "significant efforts" to comply with the minimum standards for the elimination of trafficking. Previously, Iraq received a waiver from automatic downgrading to Tier 3 (which happens if a country is "watchlisted" for three straight years) because it had developed a plan to make significant efforts to meet minimum standards for the elimination of trafficking and was devoting significant resources to that plan. On April 30,

Iraq: Politics, Governance, and Human Rights 37

2012, the COR enacted a law to facilitate elimination of trafficking in persons, both sexual and labor-related.

Media and Free Expression

While State Department and other reports attribute most of Iraq's human rights difficulties to the security situation and factional infighting, apparent curbs on free expression appear independent of such factors. One issue that troubles human rights activists is a law, passed by the COR in August 2011, called the "Journalist Rights Law." The law purports to protect journalists but left many of the provisions of Saddam-era libel and defamation laws in place. For example, the new law leaves in place imprisonment for publicly insulting the government. The State Department human rights reports have noted continuing instances of harassment and intimidation of journalists who write about corruption and the lack of government services. Much of the private media that operate is controlled by individual factions or powerful personalities. There are no overt government restrictions on access to the Internet.

In March 2012, some observers reported a setback to free expression, although instigated by militias or non-governmental groups, not the government. There were reports of 14 youths having been stoned to death by militiamen for wearing Western-style clothes and haircuts collectively known as "Emo" style. In late June 2012, the government ordered the closing of 44 new organizations that it said were operating without licenses. Included in the closure list were the BBC, Voice of America, and the U.S.-funded Radio Sawa. In early 2013, the COR adopted an "Information Crimes Law" to regulate the use of information networks, computers, and other electronic devices and systems. Human Rights Watch and other human rights groups criticized that law as "violat[ing] international standards protecting due process, freedom of speech, and freedom of association,"[35] and the COR revoked it February 2013.

Corruption

The State Department human rights report for 2013, released February 27, 2014, repeats previous years' reports that political interference and other factors such as tribal and family relationships regularly thwart the efforts of anti-corruption institutions, such as the Commission on Integrity (COI). The 2013 report says that corruption among officials across government agencies was widespread. A Joint Anti-Corruption Council, which reports to the cabinet, is tasked with implementing the government's 2010-2014 Anti-

Kenneth Katzman

Corruption Strategy. Another body is the Supreme Board of Audits, which monitors the use of government funds. The COR has its own Integrity Committee that oversees the executive branch and the governmental anti-corruption bodies. The KRG has its own separate anti-corruption institutions, including an Office of Governance and Integrity in the KRG council of ministers.

Labor Rights

A 1987 (Saddam era) labor code remains in effect, restricting many labor rights, particularly in the public sector. Although the 2005 constitution provides for the right to strike and form unions, the labor code virtually rules out independent union activity. Unions have no legal power to negotiate with employers or protect workers' rights through collective bargaining.

Religious Freedom/Situation of Religious Minorities

The Iraqi constitution provides for religious freedom and the government generally respected religious freedom, according to the State Department's report on International Religious Freedom for 2012, released May 20, 2013.[36] However, reflecting the conservative Islamic attitudes of many Iraqis, Shiite and Sunni clerics seek to enforce aspects of Islamic law and customs, sometimes coming into conflict with Iraq's generally secular traditions as well as constitutional protections. On September 13, 2012, hundreds—presumably Shiites—took to the streets in predominantly Shiite Sadr City to protest the "Innocence of Muslims" video that was produced in the United States and set off protests throughout the Middle East in September 2012. In February 2014, the cabinet adopted a Shiite "personal status law" that would permit underage marriages— reportedly an attempt by Maliki to shore up electoral support among Shiite Islamists.

Concern about religious freedom in Iraq tends to center on government treatment of religious minorities—an issue discussed extensively in the State Department International Religious Freedom report. A major concern is the safety and security of Iraq's Christian and other religious minority populations which are concentrated in northern Iraq as well as in Baghdad. These other groups include most notably the Yazidis, which number about 500,000-700,000; the Shabaks, which number about 200,000-500,000; the Sabeans, who number about 4,000; the Baha'i's that number about 2,000; and the Kakai's of Kirkuk, which number about 24,000. Since the 2003 U.S. intervention, more than half of the 1 million-1.5 million Christian population

Iraq: Politics, Governance, and Human Rights 39

that was there during Saddam's time have left. Recent estimates indicate that the Christian population of Iraq is between 400,000 and 850,000.

Violent attacks on members of the Christian community have tended to occur in waves. About 10,000 Christians in northern Iraq, fearing bombings and intimidation, fled the areas near Kirkuk during October-December 2009. On October 31, 2010, a major attack on Christians occurred when a church in Baghdad (Sayidat al-Najat Church) was besieged by militants and as many as 60 worshippers were killed. Partly as a result, Christian celebrations of Christmas 2010 were said to be subdued—following three years in which Christians had felt confident enough to celebrate that holiday openly. Several other attacks appearing to target Iraqi Christians have taken place since.

Even at the height of the U.S. military presence in Iraq, U.S. forces did not specifically protect Christian sites at all times, partly because Christian leaders do not want to appear closely allied with the United States. The State Department religious freedom report for 2011 said that during 2011, U.S. Embassy Baghdad designated a "special coordinator" to oversee U.S. funding, program implementation, and advocacy to address minority concerns.

Some Iraqi Assyrian Christians in the north blame the various attacks on them on ISIL, which operates in Nineveh Province and asserts that Christians are allies of the West. Some human rights groups allege that it is the Kurds who are committing abuses against Christians and other minorities in the Nineveh Plains, close to the KRG-controlled region. Kurdish leaders deny the allegations. To address this threat, some Iraqi Assyrian Christian groups have been advocating a "Nineveh Plains Province Solution," in which the Nineveh Plains would be turned into a self-administering region, possibly its own province. Supporters of the idea claim such a zone would pose no threat to the integrity of Iraq, but others say the plan's inclusion of a separate Christian security force could set the scene for violence and confrontation. The Iraqi government appears to have adopted a form of the plan in its January 2014 announcement that the cabinet had decided to convert the Nineveh Plains into a new province.

Funding Issues. Appropriations for FY2008 and FY2009 each earmarked $10 million in ESF to assist the Nineveh Plain Christians. The Consolidated Appropriations Act of 2010 (P.L. 111-117) made a similar provision for FY2010, although focused on Middle East minorities generally and without a specific dollar figure mandated for Iraqi Christians. The State Department International Religious Freedom report for 2012 said that the United States has funded more than $73 million for projects to support minority communities in Iraq.

Women's Rights

Iraq has a tradition of secularism and liberalism, and women's rights issues have not been as large a concern for international observers and rights groups as they have in Afghanistan or the Persian Gulf states, for example. Women serve at many levels of government, as discussed above, and are well integrated into the work force in all types of jobs and professions. By tradition, many Iraqi women wear traditional coverings but many adopt Western dress. On October 6, 2011, the COR passed legislation to lift Iraq's reservation to Article 9 of the Convention on the Elimination of All Forms of Discrimination Against Women.

Mass Graves

As is noted in the State Department report on human rights for 2012, the Iraqi government continues to uncover mass graves of Iraqi victims of the Saddam regime. This effort is under the authority of the Human Rights Ministry. The largest to date was a mass grave in Mahawil, near Hilla, that contained 3,000 bodies; the grave was discovered in 2003, shortly after the fall of the regime. In July 2012, a mass grave was discovered near Najaf, containing the bodies of about 500 Iraqi Shiites killed during the 1991 uprising against Saddam Hussein. Excavations of mass graves in Wasit and Dhi Qar provinces took place in April and May 2013, respectively.

REGIONAL RELATIONSHIPS

Iraq's neighbors, as well as the United States, have significant interest in Iraq's stability and its regional alignments. Iraq's post-Saddam Shiite leadership has affinity for Iran, which supported the Iraqi Shiites in years of struggle against Saddam. Yet, Iraq also seeks to reintegrate into the Arab fold—of which Iran is not a part—after more than 20 years of ostracism following Iraq's invasion of Kuwait in August 1990.

Iraq's reintegration into the Arab world took a large step forward with the holding of an Arab League summit in Baghdad during March 27-29, 2012. Iraq hailed the gathering as a success primarily because of the absence of major security incidents. However, only nine heads of state out of the 22 Arab League members attended, of which only one was a Persian Gulf leader (Amir Sabah al-Ahmad Al Sabah of Kuwait). On May 23-24, 2012, Iraq hosted nuclear talks between Iran and six negotiating powers.

Iraq is also sufficiently confident to begin offering assistance to other emerging Arab democracies. Utilizing its base of expertise in chemical weaponry during the Saddam Hussein regime, Iraq has provided some technical assistance to the post-Qadhafi authorities in Libya to help them clean up chemical weapons stockpiles built up by the Qadhafi regime. It donated $100,000 and provided advisers to support elections in Tunisia after its 2011 revolution.[37]

Iran

The United States has sought to limit Iran's influence over Iraq, even though many assert that it was U.S. policy that indirectly brought to power Iraqi Shiites long linked to Iran. Some argue that the withdrawal of all U.S. troops from Iraq represented a success for Iranian strategy. There has been no discernible change in Iran's influence in Iraq following the accession of the relatively moderate Iranian president Hassan Rouhani in August 2013.

Prime Minister Maliki has tried to calm fears that Iran exercises undue influence over Iraq, stressing that Iraqi nationalism resists Iranian influence. On Syria, Iraqi leaders have stressed that Iraq is neutral in the Syrian conflict and has not adopted Iran's position of openly supporting the Assad regime. Experts also note lingering distrust of Iran from the 1980-1988 Iran-Iraq war, in which an estimated 300,000 Iraqi military personnel (Shiite and Sunni) died. And Iraq's Shiite clerics also resist Iranian interference and take pride in Najaf as a more prominent center of Shiite theology and history than is the Iranian holy city of Qom.

In a December 5, 2011, op-ed in the *Washington Post*, entitled "Building a Stable Iraq," Maliki wrote:

> Iraq is a sovereign country. Our foreign policy is rooted in the fact that we do not interfere in the affairs of other countries; accordingly, we oppose foreign interference in Iraqi affairs.

On the other hand, Maliki's frequent visits to Tehran have increased U.S. concerns about his alignment with Iran. His most recent visit was on December 4, 2013, about ten days after Iran and the international community agreed to an interim deal on Iran's nuclear program. Most experts assessed the visit as an effort by Maliki to judge the potential for Iran's rebuilding of its relations with the international community. However, some observers speculated the visit might have been an effort by Maliki to arrange Tehran's support for a third term as Prime Minister.

There are indications the Shiite-led government of Iraq has sought to shield pro-Iranian militants who committed past acts of violence against U.S. forces. In May 2012, Iraqi courts acquitted and Iraq released from prison a purported Hezbollah commander, Ali Musa Daqduq, although he subsequently remained under house arrest. He had been in U.S. custody for alleged activities against U.S. forces but, under the U.S.-Iraq Security Agreement (discussed below) he was transferred to Iraqi custody in December 2011. In July 2012, U.S. officials asked Iraqi leaders to review the Daqduq case or extradite him to the United States, but Iraq released him in November 2012 and he returned to Lebanon, despite U.S. efforts to persuade Iraq to keep him there.

Still others see Iranian influence as less political than economic, raising questions about whether Iran is using Iraq to try to avoid the effects of international sanctions. Some reports say Iraq is enabling Iran's efforts by allowing it to interact with Iraq's energy sector and its banking system. In July 2012, the Treasury Department imposed sanctions on the Elaf Islamic Bank of Iraq for allegedly conducting financial transactions with the Iranian banking system that violated the Comprehensive Iran Sanctions, Accountability, and Divestment Act of 2010 (CISADA, P.L. 111-195). Those sanctions were lifted in May 2013 when Elaf reduced its involvement in Iran's financial sector. Iraq also is at least indirectly assisting U.S. policy toward Iran by supplying oil customers who, in cooperation with U.S. sanctions against Iran, are cutting back buys of oil from Iran. Iran's exports to Iraq reached about $10 billion from March 2012 to March 2013, a large increase from the $7 billion in exports in the prior one year.

The Iraqi government treatment of the population of Camp Ashraf and Camp Hurriya, camps in which over 3,500 Iranian oppositionists (People's Mojahedin Organization of Iran, PMOI) have resided, is another indicator of the government's close ties to Iran. The residents of the camps accuse the Iraqi government of recent attacks on residents.

Iran has periodically acted against other Iranian opposition groups based in Iraq. The Free Life Party (PJAK) consists of Iranian Kurds, and it is allied with the Kurdistan Workers' Party that opposes the government of Turkey. Iran has shelled purported camps of the group on several occasions. Iran is also reportedly attempting to pressure the bases and offices in Iraq of such Iranian Kurdish parties as the Kurdistan Democratic Party of Iran (KDP-I) and Komaleh.

Syria

One of the major disagreements between the United States and Iraq is on the issue of Syria. U.S. policy is to achieve the ouster of President Bashar Al Assad. Maliki's government, as noted above, stresses official "neutrality," but it is said to perceive that a post-Assad Syria would be dominated by Sunni Arabs. Maliki and his associates reportedly see the armed rebellion in Syria as aggravating the political unrest in Iraq by emboldening Iraqi Sunnis to escalate armed activities against the Maliki government.

Iraq refrained from sharp criticism of Assad for using military force against protests and it abstained on an Arab League vote in November 2011 to suspend Syria's membership. (Yemen and Lebanon were the only two "no" votes.) Perhaps to ensure Arab participation at the March 2012 Arab League summit in Baghdad, Iraq voted for a January 22, 2012, Arab League plan for a transition of power in Syria. As an indication of Iraq's policy of simultaneously engaging with the United States on the Syria issue, Foreign Minister Hoshyar Zebari has attended U.S.-led meetings of countries that are seeking Assad's ouster. At the conclusion of Maliki's meeting with President Obama on November 1, 2013, Iraq expressed support for the "Geneva II" meeting scheduled for January 22, 2014 to try to arrange a political transition in Syria.

An issue that has divided Iraq and the United States since August 2012 has been Iraq's reported permission for Iranian arms supplies to overfly Iraq en route to Syria.[38] Iraq has searched a few of these flights, particularly after specific high-level U.S. requests to do so, but has routinely allowed the aircraft to proceed after finding no arms aboard, sometimes because the Iranian aircraft had already dropped off their cargo in Syria. Instituting regular inspections of these flights was a major focus of the March 24, 2013, visit of Secretary of State Kerry to Baghdad, but the Iraqi leadership—perhaps in an effort to speed up U.S. arms deliveries—has argued that Iraq lacks the air defense and aircraft to interdict the Iranian flights. The March 2013 Secretary Kerry visit reportedly resulted in an agreement for the United States to provide Iraq with information on the likely contents of the Iranian flights in an effort to prompt Iraqi reconsideration of its position. U.S. officials said in late 2013 that the overflights appear to be diminishing in frequency.

As further indication of Maliki's support for Assad, on February 20, 2013, the Iraqi cabinet approved construction on a natural gas pipeline that will traverse Iraq and deliver Iranian gas to Syria. The project is potentially sanctionable under the Iran Sanctions Act that provides for U.S. penalties on projects that help Iran develop its energy sector, including natural gas.

Aside from official Iraqi policy, the unrest in Syria has generated a scramble among Iraqi factions to affect the outcome there. As noted above, ISIL operates on both sides of the border and each branch assists the other.[39] On March 4, 2013, suspected ISIL members on the Iraq side of the border killed 48 Syrian military personnel, and their Iraqi military escorts; the Syrians had fled a battle on the border into Iraq and were ambushed while being transported south within Iraq pending repatriation to Syria. On December 11, 2012, the United States designated a Syrian jihadist rebel group, the Al Nusrah Front, as a Foreign Terrorist Organization (FTO), asserting that it is an alias of ISIL. At the same time, as noted above, Iraqi Shiite militiamen from groups discussed above have gone to Syria to fight on behalf of the Assad regime.

The KRG appears to be assisting those Syrian Kurds who have joined the revolt against Assad. The KRG reportedly has been training Syrian Kurdish militia forces to prepare them to secure an autonomous Kurdish area if Assad loses control of the area. In August 2013, in response to fighting between the Syrian Kurds and Syrian Islamist rebel factions, Barzani threatened to deploy KRG peshmerga to help the Syrian Kurds—but no Iraqi Kurdish pershmerga have been sent. Still, many experts assert that the threat could have been the trigger for a series of bombings in normally safe Irbil on September 29, 2013. Six Kurdish security forces who guarded the attacked official buildings were killed.

Turkey

Turkey's policy toward Iraq has historically focused almost exclusively on the Iraqi Kurdish insistence on autonomy and possible push for independence—sentiments that Turkey apparently fears could embolden Kurdish oppositionists in Turkey. The anti-Turkey Kurdistan Workers' Party (PKK) has long maintained camps inside Iraq, along the border with Turkey. Turkey continues to conduct periodic bombardments and other military operations against the PKK encampments in Iraq. In October 2011, Turkey sent ground troops into northern Iraq to attack PKK bases following the killing of 24 Turkish soldiers by the PKK. However, suggesting that it has built a pragmatic relationship with the KRG, Turkey has emerged as the largest outside investor in northern Iraq and has built a close political relationship with the KRG as well.

As Turkey's relations with the KRG have deepened, relations between Turkey and the Iraqi government have worsened, although there are signs of Baghdad-Ankara reconciliation. Turkey's provision of refuge for Vice President Tariq al-Hashimi has been a source of tension; Maliki unsuccessfully sought his extradition for trial. On August 2, 2012, Turkish Foreign Minister Ahmet Davotoglu visited the disputed city of Kirkuk, prompting a rebuke from Iraq's Foreign Ministry that the visit constituted inappropriate interference in Iraqi affairs.

In an effort to improve relations, Davotoglu visited Baghdad in mid-November 2013 and, aside from meeting Maliki and other Iraqi leaders, visited Najaf and Karbala—Iraqi cities holy to Shiites. That visit appeared intended to signal Turkish evenhandedness with regard to sectarian disputes in Iraq, as well as a willingness to minimize any dispute over KRG oil exports through Turkey. During that visit, Maliki reportedly proposed the two develop a "north-south" energy corridor through which Iraqi energy exports could flow to Europe via Turkey. Davotoglu apparently did not commit or object to that proposal. Deputy Assistant Secretary of State Brett McGurk testified before the House Foreign Affairs Committee on November 13, 2013, that the United States supports that concept as well as another export pipeline that would carry Iraqi oil to Jordan's Red Sea outlet at Aqaba.

Gulf States

Iraq has reduced tensions with several of the Sunni-led Persian Gulf states who have not fully accommodated themselves to the fact that Iraq is now dominated by Shiite factions. All of the Gulf states were represented at the March 27-29, 2012, Arab League summit in Baghdad summit but Amir Sabah of Kuwait was the only Gulf head of state to attend. Qatar sent a very low-level delegation, which it said openly was meant as a protest against the Iraqi government's treatment of Sunni Arab factions.

Saudi Arabia had been widely criticized by Iraqi leaders because it has not opened an embassy in Baghdad, a move Saudi Arabia pledged in 2008 and which the United States has long urged. This issue faded somewhat after February 2012, when Saudi Arabia announced that it had named its ambassador to Jordan, Fahd al-Zaid, to serve as a non-resident ambassador to Iraq concurrently— although still not opening an embassy in Baghdad. The other Gulf countries have opened embassies and all except the UAE have appointed full ambassadors to Iraq.

46 Kenneth Katzman

The government of Bahrain, which is mostly Sunni, also fears that Iraq might work to empower Shiite oppositionists who have demonstrated for a constitutional monarchy during 2011. Ayatollah Sistani is revered by many Bahraini Shiites, and Iraqi Shiites have demonstrated in solidarity with the Bahraini opposition, but there is no evidence that Iraq has had any direct role in the Bahrain unrest.

Kuwait

The relationship with Kuwait has always been considered difficult to resolve because of the legacy of the 1990 Iraqi invasion. However, greater acceptance of the Iraqi government was demonstrated by the visit of Kuwait's then prime minister to Iraq on January 12, 2011. Maliki subsequently visited Kuwait on February 16, 2011, and, as noted above, the Amir of Kuwait attended the Arab League summit in Baghdad in March 2012. The Prime Minister of Kuwait visited in mid-June 2013, which led to an agreement to remove the outstanding issues of Kuwaiti persons and property missing from the Iraqi invasion from U.N. Security Council (Chapter VII) supervision to oversight by UNAMI under Chapter VI of the U.N. Charter. This transition was implemented by U.N. Security Council Resolution 2107 of June 27, 2013. The two countries have also resolved the outstanding issues of maintenance of border demarcation. In late October 2013, the Iraqi cabinet voted to allow Kuwait to open consulates in Basra and Irbil.

The resolution of these issues follows the U.N. Security Council passage on December 15, 2010, of Resolutions 1956, 1957, and 1958. These resolutions had the net effect of lifting most Saddam-era sanctions on Iraq, although the U.N.-run reparations payments process remains intact (and deducts 5% from Iraq's total oil revenues). As of the end of December 2012, a U.N. Compensation Commission set up under Security Council Resolution 687 has paid $38.8 billion to claimants from the 1990-1991 Iraqi occupation of Kuwait, with an outstanding balance of $13.6 billion to be paid by April 2015.

U.S. MILITARY WITHDRAWAL AND POST-2011 POLICY

A complete U.S. military withdrawal from Iraq by the end of 2011 was a stipulation of the November 2008 U.S.-Iraq Security Agreement (SA), which took effect on January 1, 2009. Following the SA's entry into force, President Obama, on February 27, 2009, outlined a U.S. troop drawdown plan that provided for a drawdown of U.S. combat brigades by the end of August 2010,

Iraq: Politics, Governance, and Human Rights

with a residual force of 50,000 primarily for training the Iraq Security Forces, to remain until the end of 2011. An interim benchmark in the SA was the June 30, 2009, withdrawal of U.S. combat troops from Iraq's cities. These withdrawal deadlines were adhered to.

Question of Whether U.S. Forces Would Remain Beyond 2011

During 2011, with the deadline for a complete U.S. withdrawal approaching, fears of expanded Iranian influence, and perceived deficiencies in Iraq's nearly 800,000 member security forces caused U.S. officials to seek to revise the SA to keep some U.S. troops in Iraq after 2011. Some U.S. experts feared the rifts among major ethnic and sectarian communities were still wide enough that Iraq could still become a "failed state" unless some U.S. troops remained. U.S. officials emphasized that the ongoing ISF weaknesses centered on lack of ability to defend Iraq's airspace and borders. Iraqi comments that it would be unable to execute full external defense until 2020-2024, reinforced those who asserted that a U.S. force presence was still needed.[40] Renegotiating the SA to allow for a continued U.S. troop presence required discussions with the Iraqi government and a ratification vote of the Iraqi COR.

Several high-level U.S. visits and statements urged the Iraqis to consider extending the U.S. troop presence. Maliki told visiting Speaker of the House John Boehner during an April 16, 2011, visit to Baghdad that Iraq would welcome U.S. training and arms after that time.[41] Subsequent to Boehner's visit, Maliki, anticipating that a vote of the COR would be needed for any extension, stated that a request for U.S. troops might be made if there were a "consensus" among political blocs (which he later defined as at least 70% concurrence).[42] This appeared to be an effort to isolate the Sadr faction, the most vocal opponent of a continuing U.S. presence. On August 3, 2011, major factions gave Maliki their backing to negotiate an SA extension. In September 2011, a figure of about 15,000 remaining U.S. troops, reflecting recommendations of the U.S. military, was being widely discussed.[43] The *New York Times* reported on September 7, 2011, that the Administration was considering proposing to Iraq to retain only about 3,000-4,000 forces, mostly in a training role.[44] Many experts criticized that figure as too low to carry out intended missions.

Decision on Full Withdrawal

The difficulty in the negotiations—partly a function of Sadrist opposition to a post-2011 U.S. presence—clarified on October 5, 2011 when Iraq issued a statement that Iraq would not extend the legal protections contained in the existing SA. That stipulation failed to meet the Defense Department requirements that U.S. soldiers not be subject to prosecution under Iraq's constitution and its laws. On October 21, 2011, President Obama announced that the United States and Iraq had agreed that, in accordance with the November 2008 Security Agreement (SA), all U.S. troops would leave Iraq at the end of 2011. With the formal end of the U.S. combat mission on August 31, 2010, U.S. forces dropped to 47,000, and force levels dropped steadily from August to December 2011. The last U.S. troop contingent crossed into Kuwait on December 18, 2011.

The subsequent Sunni unrest and violence has caused some to argue that the Administration should have pressed Iraqi leaders harder to allow a U.S. contingent to remain. Those who support the Administration view say that political crisis was likely no matter when the United States withdrew and that it is the responsibility of the Iraqis to resolve their differences.

Post-2011 U.S.-Iraq Security Relationship

After the withdrawal announcement, senior U.S. officials stated that the United States would be able to continue to help Iraq secure itself using programs commonly provided for other countries. Administration officials stressed that the U.S. political and residual security-related presence would be sufficient to exert influence and leverage to ensure that Iraq remained stable, allied to the United States, continuing to move toward full democracy, and economically growing and vibrant. At the time of the withdrawal, there were about 16,000 total U.S. personnel in Iraq, about half of which were contractors. Of the contractors, most were on missions to protect the U.S. Embassy and consulates, and other U.S. personnel and facilities throughout Iraq.

Office of Security Cooperation-Iraq (OSC-I)

The Office of Security Cooperation—Iraq (OSC-I), operating under the authority of the U.S. Ambassador to Iraq, is the primary Iraq-based U.S. institution that interacts with the Iraqi military—primarily by administering the Foreign Military Sales (FMS) programs (U.S. arms sales to Iraq). OSC-I,

Iraq: Politics, Governance, and Human Rights

funded with the Foreign Military Financing (FMF) funds discussed in the aid table below, is the largest U.S. security cooperation office in the world. It works out of the U.S. Embassy in Baghdad and five other locations around Iraq (Kirkuk Regional Airport Base, Tikrit, Besmaya, Umm Qasr, and Taji).

The total OCS-I personnel numbers over 3,500, but the vast majority are security and support personnel, most of which are contractors. Of the staff, about 175 are U.S. military personnel and an additional 45 are Defense Department civilians. About 46 members of the staff administer the Foreign Military Sales (FMS) program and other security assistance programs such as the International Military Education and Training (IMET) program. Since 2005, DOD has administered 231 U.S.-funded FMS cases totaling $2.5 billion, and 201 Iraq-funded cases totaling $7.9 billion. There are a number of other purchase requests initiated by Iraq that, if they all move forward, would bring the estimated value of all Iraq FMS cases to nearly $25 billion.[45]

Major Arms Sales

The United States has been selling substantial quantities of arms to Iraq, both before and after the U.S. withdrawal, and before and after the 2014 ISIL-led uprising. A large part of the pre-U.S. withdrawal arms sale program to Iraq was for 140 M1A1 Abrams tanks. Deliveries began in August 2010 and were completed in August 2012. The tanks cost about $860 million, of which $800 million was paid out of Iraq's national funds. A year after the withdrawal, in December 2012, the U.S. Navy delivered two support ships to Iraq, which will assist Iraq's fast-attack and patrol boats that secure its offshore oil platforms and other coastal and offshore locations. The United States also has sold Iraq equipment that its security forces can use to restrict the ability of insurgent and terrorist groups to move contraband across Iraq's borders and checkpoints (RAPISCAN system vehicles), at a cost of about $600 million. Some refurbished air defense guns were provided gratis as excess defense articles (EDA). Since late 2013, nearly 600 HELLFIRE missiles for use on Iraq's propeller-driven aircraft, have been rushed to Iraq in the context of the ISIL-led insurrection, as discussed above.

F-16s. The largest FMS case is the sale of 36 U.S.-made F-16 combat aircraft to Iraq, notified to Congress in two equal tranches, the latest of which was made on December 12, 2011 (Transmittal No. 11-46). The total value of the sale of 36 F-16s is up to $6.5 billion when all parts, training, and weaponry are included. The first deliveries of the aircraft are scheduled for September 2014, although Iraqi officials—including Maliki during his visit to Washington, DC, in late October 2013—say that accelerating the deliveries would facilitate Iraqi efforts to inspect Iranian overflights to Syria. Some experts and Iraqi politicians, particularly the Kurds, called for withholding the F-16 deliveries unless Maliki recommits to power-sharing with Sunni and Kurdish leaders, loosens ties to Iran, and fully cooperates with U.S. policy on Syria. Iraq's Kurdish leaders have long argued that Maliki could use the F-16s against domestic opponents. The late 2013-early 2014 ISIL uprising have virtually ensured the delivery will go forward.

Apache Attack Helicopters and Stingers. In order to secure its airspace and to combat ISIL, in 2013 Iraq requested to purchase from the United States the Integrated Air Defense System and Apache attack helicopters, with a total sale value of about $10 billion.[46] The sale of the Air Defense system was notified to Congress on August 5, 2013, with a value of $2.4 billion, and includes 681 Stinger shoulder held units, 3 Hawk anti-aircraft batteries, and other equipment. On that day, and in the preceding week, DSCA notified about $2.3 billion worth of other sales to Iraq of Stryker nuclear, chemical, and biological equipment reconnaissance vehicles, 12 Bell helicopters, the Mobile Troposcatter Radio System, and maintenance support. The provision of Apaches involves the lease of six of the helicopters, with an estimated cost of about $1.37 billion, and the sale of 24 more, with an estimated value of $4.8 billion. The six to be leased might arrive later in 2014 and the 24 to be sold would be delivered by 2017. As noted above, the provision of the Apaches was held up by some in Congress until the 2014 ISIL-led insurrection that created an apparent acute need for the system.

Drones. The United States has sold Iraq several unmanned aerial vehicles that perform surveillance, for example of ISIL camps in western Anbar Province. The systems provided including ten "Scaneagle" aerial vehicles.[47]

Non-U.S. Sales

Perhaps to hedge against a potential U.S. cutoff, Iraq seeks to diversify its arms supplies. Maliki visited Russia on October 8, 2012, and signed deals for Russian arms worth about $4.2 billion. In early November 2013, Russia delivered four Mi-35 attack helicopters to Iraq. Iraq might also buy MiG fighter jets in the future, according to press reports. In mid-October 2012, Iraq agreed to buy 28 Czech-made military aircraft, a deal valued at about $1 billion.[48] On December 12, 2013, South Korea signed a deal to export 24 FA-50 light fighter jets to Iraq at an estimated cost of $1.1 billion; the aircraft will be delivered between 2015 and 2016.[49]

Police Development Program

A separate program is the Police Development Program, the largest program that transitioned from DOD to State Department lead, using International Narcotics and Law Enforcement (INCLE) funds. However, Iraq's drive to emerge from U.S. tutelage produced apparent Iraqi disinterest in the PDP. By late 2012, it consisted of only 36 advisers, about 10% of what was envisioned as an advisory force of 350, and it is being phased out entirely during 2013. Two facilities built with over $200 million in U.S. funds (Baghdad Police College Annex and part of the U.S. consulate in Basra) are to be turned over the Iraqi government by December 2012. Some press reports say there is Administration consideration of discontinuing the program entirely.[50]

Other Security Assistance and Training Programs

In addition to administering arms sales to Iraq, OSC-I conducts train and assist programs for the Iraq military. Because the United States and Iraq have not concluded a Status of Forces Agreement (SOFA) document that would grant legal immunities to U.S. military personnel, the 160 OSC-I personnel involved in these programs are mostly contractors. They train Iraq's forces on counterterrorism and naval and air defense. Some are "embedded" with Iraqi forces as trainers not only tactically, but at the institutional level by advising Iraqi security ministries and its command structure.

As Sunni unrest has increased since early 2012, Iraq has sought additional security cooperation with the United States. On August 19, 2012, en route to a visit to Iraq, Chairman of the Joint Chiefs of Staff General Martin Dempsey said that "I think [Iraqi leaders] recognize their capabilities may require yet more additional development and I think they're reaching out to us to see if we can help them with that."[51] Aside from accelerated delivery of U.S. arms to be sold,[52] Iraq reportedly expressed to Dempsey interest in expanded U.S. training of the ISF and joint exercises. After the Dempsey visit, it was reported that, at the request of Iraq, a unit of Army Special Operations forces had deployed to Iraq to advise on counterterrorism and help with intelligence, presumably against AQ-I/ISIL.[53] (These forces presumably are operating under a limited SOFA or related understanding crafted for this purpose.) Other reports suggest that Central Intelligence Agency (CIA) paramilitary forces had, as of late 2012, largely taken over some of the DOD mission of helping Iraqi counterterrorism forces (Counter-Terrorism Service, CTS) against ISIL in western Iraq.[54] Part of the reported CIA mission is to also work against ISIL in Syria.

Kenneth Katzman

During December 5-6, 2012, Under Secretary of Defense for Policy James Miller and acting Under Secretary of State for International Security Rose Gottemoeller visited Iraq and a Memorandum of Understanding (MOU) was signed with acting Defense Minister Sadoun Dulaymi. The five year MOU provides for:

- high level U.S.-Iraq military exchanges
- professional military education cooperation
- counter-terrorism cooperation
- the development of defense intelligence capabilities
- joint exercises

The MOU appeared to address many of the issues that have hampered OSC-I from performing the its mission to its full potential. The MOU also reflects some of the more recent ideas put forward, such as joint exercises.

The concept of enhanced U.S.-Iraq cooperation gained further consideration in mid-2013. In June 2013, General Dempsey, said that the United States was ooking for ways to improve the military capabilities of Iraq and Lebanon, two countries extensively affected by the Syria conflict. He added that enhanced assistance could involve dispatching training teams and accelerating sales of weapons and equipment. During his August 2013 visit to Washington D.C, conducted primarily to attend meetings of the U.S.-Iraq Political and Diplomatic Joint Coordination Committee (JCC), Foreign Minister Hoshyar Zebari indicated that Iraq wants to expand security cooperation with the United States to enhance ISF capability. His visit came several weeks after a major insurgent attack on July 21, 2013, against the Abu Ghraib prison outside Baghdad that caused many experts to say that the lapsing of U.S.-Iraq security cooperation had caused ISF proficiency to deteriorate.

During his November 1, 2013, meeting with President Obama, Maliki reportedly discussed enhanced security cooperation, including expanded access to U.S. intelligence, with U.S. officials, including President Obama and Secretary of Defense Hagel.[55] The joint statement issued at the conclusion of Maliki's meeting with President Obama did not specify any U.S. commitments to this level of cooperation, but did express a "shared assessment of al Qaida affiliated groups threatening Iraq." The joint statement indicated that Iraq has a "comprehensive strategy" to isolate AQ-I/ISIL through "coordinated security, economic, and political measures," appearing to adopt U.S. urgings for a political solution in addition to security measures targeted at militant groups in

Iraq. Prior to the November 1 meeting, six Senators signed a letter to President Obama expressing concerns about broadening strategic relations with Iraq in light of Maliki's policies toward his domestic opponents. Some members of the Senate Foreign Relations Committee and the House Foreign Affairs Committee met with Maliki during his visit and reportedly expressed similar concerns to him directly.[56]

In the context of the ISIL-led insurrection in early 2014, OSC-I has stepped up "non-operational" training with Iraqi counterterrorism units, as testified by Deputy Assistant Secretary McGurk on February 5, 2014. If a SOFA is agreed, some of these missions could be performed by U.S. military personnel, presumably augmenting the effectiveness of the programs. However, there has been no direct U.S. combat assistance to the ISF in the context of the 2014 ISIL-led insurrection. On January 5, 2014, Secretary of State Kerry pointedly ruled out any deployment of U.S. troops to Iraq, saying that it would be left to the Iraqis themselves to handle the crisis. Instead, the U.S. military says it has sought to integrate the ISF into regional security exercises and structures that can augment the ISF's proficiency. The United States has arranged Iraq's participation in the regional Eager Lion military exercise series in Jordan. Iraq also participated in the U.S.-led international mine countermeasures exercise off Bahrain in 2013. In July 2013, the United States convened a strategic dialogue that includes Iraq, Jordan, and the United Arab Emirates, and Egypt joined the subsequent session of the dialogue the week of November 18, 2013.

Regional Reinforcement Capability

Should the United States decide to intervene directly to assist Iraq, it retains a significant capability in the Persian Gulf region to do so. The United States has about 35,000 military personnel in the region, including about 10,000 mostly U.S. Army forces in Kuwait, a portion of which are combat ready rather than purely support forces. There is also prepositioned armor there and in Qatar. There are about 7,000 mostly Air Force personnel in Qatar; 5,000 mostly Navy personnel in Bahrain; and about 5,000 mostly Air Force and Navy in the UAE, with very small numbers in Saudi Arabia and Oman. The rest are part of at least one aircraft carrier task force in or near the Gulf at any given time. The forces are in the Gulf under bilateral defense cooperation agreements with all six Gulf Cooperation Council (GCC) states that give the United States access to military facilities to station forces and preposition some heavy armor.

The Diplomatic and Economic Relationship

In his withdrawal announcement, President Obama stated that, through U.S. assistance programs, the United States would be able to continue to develop all facets of the bilateral relationship with Iraq and help strengthen its institutions.[57] The bilateral civilian relationship was the focus of a visit to Iraq by Vice President Biden in early December 2011, just prior to the December 12, 2011, Maliki visit to the United States.

The cornerstone of the bilateral relationship is the Strategic Framework Agreement (SFA). The SFA, signed and entered into effect at the same time as the SA, presents a framework for long-term U.S.-Iraqi relations, and is intended to help orient Iraq's politics and its economy toward the West and the developed nations, and reduce its reliance on Iran or other regional states. The SFA sets up a Higher Coordination Committee (HCC) and as an institutional framework for high-level U.S.-Iraq meetings, and subordinate Joint Coordinating Committees. No meeting of the HCC was held in 2012, but Foreign Minister Zebari's August 2013 visit was in conjunction with one of the JCCs. During Maliki's October 29-November 1, 2013, visit, the HCC was convened—the fourth meeting of the HCC since the SFA was signed.

The SFA provides for the following (among other provisions):

- U.S.-Iraq cooperation "based on mutual respect," and that the United States will not use Iraqi facilities to launch any attacks against third countries, and will not seek permanent bases.
- U.S. support for Iraqi democracy and support for Iraq in regional and international organizations.
- U.S.-Iraqi dialogue to increase Iraq's economic development, including through the Dialogue on Economic Cooperation and a Trade and Investment Framework Agreement (TIFA). The United States and Iraq announced on March 6, 2013, that a bilateral TIFA had been finalized.
- Promotion of Iraq's development of its electricity, oil, and gas sector.
- U.S.-Iraq dialogue on agricultural issues and promotion of Iraqi participation in agricultural programs run by the U.S. Department of Agriculture and USAID.
- Cultural cooperation through several exchange programs, such as the Youth Exchange and Study Program and the International Visitor Leadership Program. The joint statement following Maliki's meeting with President Obama said that nearly 1,000 Iraqi students were studying in the United States and that the two sides had a "shared

commitment" to increase than number and to increase cultural, artistic, and scientific exchanges.

State Department-run aid programs are intended to fulfill the objectives of the SFA, according to State Department budget documents. These programs are implemented mainly through the Economic Support Fund, and the State Department budget justification for foreign operations for FY2014 indicates that most U.S. economic aid to Iraq for FY2014 will go to programs to promote democracy, adherence to international standards of human rights, rule of law, and conflict resolution. Programs funded by the State Department Bureau of International Narcotics and Law Enforcement (INL) will focus on rule of law, moving away from previous use of INL funds for police training. Funding will continue for counterterrorism operations (NADR funds), and for anti-corruption initiatives.

U.S. officials stress that the United States does not bear the only burden for implementing the programs above, in light of the fact that Iraq is now a major oil exporter. For programs run by USAID in Iraq, Iraq matches one-for-one the U.S. funding contribution.

The State Department as Lead Agency

Virtually all of the responsibility for conducting the bilateral relationship falls on the State Department, which became the lead U.S. agency in Iraq as of October 1, 2011. With the transition completed, the State Department announced on March 9, 2012, that its "Office of the Iraq Transition Coordinator" had closed. In July 2011, as part of the transition to State leadership in Iraq, the United States formally opened consulates in Basra, Irbil, and Kirkuk. An embassy branch office was considered for Mosul but cost and security issues kept the U.S. facility there limited to a diplomatic office. The Kirkuk consulate closed at the end of July 2012 due in part to security concerns, as well as to save costs. As reflected in its FY2014 budget request, the State Department is planning to replace the U.S. consulate in Irbil with a New Consulate Compound in Irbil. The FY2014 Consolidated Appropriation, P.L. 113-76 provides $250 million for that purpose. The Ambassador in Iraq is Robert Stephen Beecroft, who was confirmed by the Senate in September 2012.

The size and cost of the U.S. civilian presence in Iraq is undergoing reduction. U.S. officials said in mid-2012 that the U.S. Embassy in Baghdad, built at a cost of about $750 million, carries too much staff relative to the needed mission. From nearly 17,000 personnel at the time of the completion of the U.S. withdrawal at the end of 2011, the number of U.S. personnel in Iraq fell to about 10,000 in mid-2013 and has fallen to about 5,500 at the end of 2013.[58] Of the U.S. personnel in Iraq, about 1,000 are U.S. diplomats or other civilian employees of the U.S. government.[59] There have been no U.S. casualties in Iraq since the troop withdrawal.

As shown in **Table 4** below (in the note), the State Department request for operations (which includes costs for the Embassy as well as other facilities and all personnel in Iraq) is about $1.18 billion for FY2014—less than half the $2.7 billion requested for FY2013, and down 66% from the $3.6 billion provided in FY2012. FY2012 was considered a "transition year" to State Department leadership, requiring high start-up costs.

No Sanctions Impediments

As the U.S.-Iraq relationship matures, some might focus increasingly on U.S.-Iraq trade and U.S. investment in Iraq. After the fall of Saddam Hussein, all U.S. economic sanctions against Iraq were lifted. Iraq was removed from the "terrorism list," and the Iraq Sanctions Act (Sections 586-586J of P.L. 101-513), which codified a U.S. trade embargo imposed after Iraq's invasion of Kuwait, was terminated. As noted above in the section on the Gulf states, in December 2010, a series of U.N. Security Council resolutions removed most remaining "Chapter VII" U.N. sanctions against Iraq, with the exception of the reparations payments to Kuwait. The lifting of U.N. sanctions allows any country to sell arms to Iraq. Iraq still is required to comply with international proliferation regimes that bar it from reconstituting Saddam-era weapons of mass destruction programs. On October 24, 2012, Iraq demonstrated its commitment to compliance with these restrictions by signing the "Additional Protocol" of the Nuclear Non-Proliferation Treaty. Because sanctions have been lifted, there are no impediments to U.S. business dealings with Iraq.

Table 3. March 2010 COR Election: Final, Certified Results by Province

Province	Elected Seats in COR	Results
Baghdad	68	Maliki: 26 seats; Iraqiyya: 24 seats; INA: 17 seats; minority reserved: 2 seats
Nineveh (Mosul)	31	Iraqiiya: 20; Kurdistan Alliance: 8; INA: 1; Accordance: 1; Unity(Bolani): 1; minority reserved: 3
Qadisiyah	11	Maliki: 4; INA: 5; Iraqiyya: 2
Muthanna	7	Maliki: 4; INA: 3

Iraq: Politics, Governance, and Human Rights

Province	Elected Seats in COR	Results
Dohuk	10	Kurdistan Alliance: 9; other Kurdish lists: 1; minority reserved: 1
Basra	24	Maliki: 14; INA: 7; Iraqiyya: 3
Anbar	14	Iraqiyya: 11; Unity (Bolani): 1; Accordance: 2
Karbala	10	Maliki: 6; INA: 3; Iraqiyya: 1
Wasit	11	Maliki: 5; INA: 4; Iraqiyya: 2
Dhi Qar	18	Maliki: 8; INA: 9; Iraqiyya: 1
Sulaymaniyah	17	Kurdistan Alliance: 8; other Kurds: 9
Kirkuk (Tamim)	12	Iraqiyya: 6; Kurdistan Alliance: 6
Babil	16	Maliki: 8; INA: 5; Iraqiyya: 3
Irbil	14	Kurdistan Alliance: 10; other Kurds: 4
Najaf	12	Maliki: 7; INA: 5
Diyala	13	Iraqiyya: 8; INA: 3; Maliki: 1; Kurdistan Alliance: 1
Salahuddin	12	Iraqiyya: 8; Unity (Bolani): 2; Accordance: 2
Maysan	10	Maliki: 4; INA: 6
Total Seats	**325** (310 elected + 8 minority reserved + 7 compensatory)	Iraqiyya: 89 + 2 compensatory = 91
		Maliki: 87 + 2 compensatory = 89
		INA: 68 + 2 compensatory = 70 (of which about 40 Sadrist)
		Kurdistan Alliance: 42 +1 compensatory = 43
		Unity (Bolani): 4
		Accordance: 6
		other Kurdish: 14
		minority reserved: 8

Source: Iraqi Higher Election Commission, March 26, 2010.
Total seats do not add to 325 total seats in the COR due to some uncertainties in allocations.

Table 4. U.S. Assistance to Iraq: FY2003-FY2015
(appropriations/allocations in millions of $)

	FY '03	04	05	06	07	08	09	10	11	12	Total 03-12	FY 13	FY 14	FY15 (request)
IRRF	2,475	18,389	—	10	—	—	—	—	—	—	20,874			
ESF	—	—	—	1,535.4	1,677	429	541.5	382.5	325.7	250	5,140	72.3	72.3	22.5
Democracy Fund	—	—	—	—	250	75	—	—	—	—	325			
IFTA (Treasury Dept. Asst.)	—	—	—	13.0	2.8	—	—	—	—	—	15.8			
NADR	—	—	3.6	—	18.4	20.4	35.5	30.3	29.8	32	170	31.1	31.1	23.86
Refugee Accounts (MRA and ERMA)	39.6	.1	—	—	78.3	278	260	316	280	—	1,100			
IDA	22	—	7.1	.3	45	85	51	42	17	—	269			
Other USAID Funds	470	—	—	—	—	23.8	—	—	—	—	494			
INCLE	—	—	—	91.4	170	85	20	702	114.6	137	1,320	13.5	13.5	11.0
FMF	—	—	—	—	—	—	—	—	—	850	850	471.3	471.3	250
IMET	—	1.2	—	—	1.1	—	2	2	1.7	2	10	1.1	1.7	1.4
DOD—ISF Funding	—	—	5,391	3,007	5,542	3,000	1,000	1,000	1,155	—	20,095			
DOD—Iraq Army	51.2	—	210	—	—	—	—	—	—	—	261			
DOD—CERP	—	140	718	708	750	996	339	263	44.0	—	3,958			

	FY '03	04	05	06	07	08	09	10	11	12	Total 03-12	FY 13	FY 14	FY15 (request)
DOD—Oil Repair	802	—	—	—	—	—	—	—	—	—	802			
DOD—Business Support	—	—	—	—	50.0	50.0	74.0	—	—	—	174			
Total	**3,859**	**18,548**	**6,329**	**5,365**	**8,584**	**5,042**	**2,323**	**2,738**	**1,968**	**1,519**	**56,259**	**589.4**	**590**	**308.7**

Sources: FY2014 Consolidated Appropriation (P.L. 113-76); State Department FY2015 budget documents, and CRS calculations.

Notes: Table prepared by Curt Tarnoff, Specialist in Foreign Affairs, This table does not contain agency operational costs, except where these are embedded in the larger reconstruction accounts. IMET=International Military Education and Training; IRRF=Iraq Relief and Reconstruction Fund; INCLE=International Narcotics and Law Enforcement Fund; ISF=Iraq Security Force; NADR=Nonproliferation, Anti-Terrorism, Demining and Related: ESF=Economic Support Fund; IDA=International Disaster Assistance; FMF=Foreign Military Financing; ISF= Iraqi Security Forces. FY2015 request includes $250 million to construct new consulate compound in Basra to support Iraq's oil and oil export industry expansion.

Table 5. Recent Democracy Assistance to Iraq
(in millions of current $)

	FY2009	FY2010 (act.)	FY2011	FY2012
Rule of Law and Human Rights	32.45	33.3	16.5	29.75
Good Governance	143.64	117.40	90.33	100.5
Political Competition/ Consensus-Building	41.00	52.60	30.00	16.25
Civil Society	87.53	83.6	32.5	55.5
Totals	**304.62**	**286.9**	**169.33**	**202.0**

Source: Congressional Budget Justification, March 2011. Figures for these accounts are included in the overall assistance figures presented in the table above. FY2013 and FY2014 ESF and INCLE-funded programs focus extensively on democracy and governance, rule of law, and anti-corruption.

Table 6. Election Results (January and December 2005)

Bloc/Party	Seats (Jan. 05)	Seats (Dec. 05)
United Iraqi Alliance (UIA, Shiite Islamist). 85 seats after departure of Fadilah (15 seats) and Sadr faction (28 seats) in 2007. Islamic Supreme Council of Iraq of Abd al-Aziz al-Hakim has 30; Da'wa Party (25 total: Maliki faction, 12, and Anizi faction, 13); independents (30).	140	128
Kurdistan Alliance—KDP (24); PUK (22); independents (7)	75	53
Iraqis List (secular, Allawi); added Communist and other mostly Sunni parties for Dec. vote.	40	25
Iraq Accord Front. Main Sunni bloc; not in Jan. vote. Consists of Iraqi Islamic Party (IIP, Tariq al-Hashimi, 26 seats); National Dialogue Council of Khalaf Ulayyan (7); General People's Congress of Adnan al-Dulaymi (7); independents (4).	—	44
National Iraqi Dialogue Front (Sunni, led by former Baathist Saleh al-Mutlak) Not in Jan. 2005 vote.	—	11
Kurdistan Islamic Group (Islamist Kurd) (votes with Kurdistan Alliance)	2	5
Iraqi National Congress (Chalabi). Was part of UIA list in Jan. 05 vote	—	0

Iraq: Politics, Governance, and Human Rights

Bloc/Party	Seats (Jan. 05)	Seats (Dec. 05)
Iraqis Party (Yawar, Sunni); Part of Allawi list in Dec. vote	5	—
Iraqi Turkomen Front (Turkomen, Kirkuk-based, pro-Turkey)	3	1
National Independent and Elites (Jan)/Risalyun (Message, Dec.) pro-Sadr	3	2
People's Union (Communist, non-sectarian); on Allawi list in Dec. vote	2	—
Islamic Action (Shiite Islamist, Karbala)	2	0
National Democratic Alliance (non-sectarian, secular)	1	—
Rafidain National List (Assyrian Christian)	1	1
Liberation and Reconciliation Gathering (Umar al-Jabburi, Sunni, secular)	1	3
Ummah (Nation) Party. (Secular, Mithal al-Alusi, former INC activist)	0	1
Yazidi list (small Kurdish, heterodox religious minority in northern Iraq)	—	1

Notes: Number of polling places: January: 5,200; December: 6,200; Eligible voters: 14 million in January election; 15 million in October referendum and December; Turnout: January: 58% (8.5 million votes)/ October: 66% (10 million)/December: 75% (12 million).

End Notes

[1] Text, in English, is at http://www.constitution.org/cons/iraq/TAL.html.

[2] Text of the Iraqi constitution is at http://www.washingtonpost.com/wp-dyn/content/article/2005/10/12/ AR2005101201450.html.

[3] "The Iraq Study Group Report." Vintage Books, 2006. The Iraq Study Group was funded by the conference report on P.L. 109-234, FY2006 supplemental, which provided $1 million to the U.S. Institute of Peace for operations of an Iraq Study Group. The legislation did not specify the Group's exact mandate or its composition.

[4] Analysis of Iraq expert Reidar Visser. "The Hashemi Veto." http://gulfanalysis.wordpress.com/2009/11/18/the-hashemi-veto/.

[5] Fadel, Leila and Karen DeYoung. "Iraqi Leaders Crack Political Deadlock." *Washington Post*, November 11, 2010.

[6] An antecedent of AQ-I/ISIL was named by the United States as a Foreign Terrorist Organization (FTO) in March 2004 and the designation applies to AQ-I/ISIL.

[7] Michael Schmidt and Eric Schmitt. "Leaving Iraq, U.S. Fears New Surge of Qaeda Terror." *New York Times*, November 6, 2011.

[8] Michael Knights. "Rebuilding Iraq's Counterterrorism Capabilities." *Washington Institute for Near East Policy*, July 31, 2013.

[9] Ben Van Heuvelen. "Al Qaeda-Linked Group Gaining Ground in Iraq." *Washington Post*, December 8, 2013.

[10] Eileen Sullivan. "Official: Al-Qaida in Iraq Strongest Since 2006." Associated Press, November 14, 2013.

[11] Prime Minister Maliki address at the U.S. Institute of Peace. Attended by the author, October 31, 2013.

[12] The acronym stands for Jaysh al-Rijal al-Tariq al-Naqshabandi, which translated means Army of the Men of the Naqshabandi Order.

[13] Liz Sly. "Iran-Tied Group Is On Rise in Iraq." Washington Post, February 19, 2013.

[14] Michael Knights. "Iraq's Never-Ending Security Crisis." BBC News, October 3, 2013.

[15] Abigail Hauslohner. "Iraqi Shiites Take Up the Cudgels for Syrian Government." *Washington Post*, May 27, 2013.

[16] For more information on Kurd-Baghdad disputes, see CRS Report RS22079, *The Kurds in Post-Saddam Iraq*, by Kenneth Katzman.

[17] Interview with Masoud Barzani by Hayder al-Khoie on Al-Hurra television network. April 6, 2012.

[18] Testimony of Deputy Assistant Secretary of State Brett McGurk before the House Foreign Affairs Committee. November 13, 2013.

[19] "Managing Arab-Kurd Tensions in Northern Iraq After the Withdrawal of U.S. Troops." Rand Corporation, 2011.

[20] Much of the dispute centers on differing interpretations of a 1976 Iraq- Turkey treaty, which was extended in 2010, and which defines "Iraq" (for purposes of oil issues) as the "Ministry of Oil of the Republic of Iraq." See: "analysis: Iraq-Turkey Treaty Restricts Kurdistan Exports." Iraq Oil Report, April 18, 2014.

[21] Jane Arraf. "Iraq's Unity Tested by Rising Tensions Over Oil-Rich Kurdish Region." *Christian Science Monitor*, May 4, 2012.

[22] Sadun Dulaymi, a Sunni Arab, is acting Defense Minister; Falih al-Fayad, a Shiite, is acting Minister of State for National Security; and Adnan al-Asadi, another Shiite, is acting Interior Minister.

[23] Parker, Ned and Salar Jaff. "Electoral Ruling Riles Maliki's Rivals." *Los Angeles Times*, January 23, 2011.

[24] Tim Arango. "Iraq's Prime Minister Gains More Power After Political Crisis." *New York Times*, February 28, 2012.

[25] "Embattled Iraqi PM Holding On To Power for Now." Associated Press, June 12, 2012.

[26] Author conversations with Human Rights Watch researchers, March 2013.

[27] Duraid Adnan. "18 Are Found Shot to Death After Abduction in Baghdad." *New York Times*, November 30, 2013.

[28] Reidar Vissar. "Provincial Powers Revisions, Elections Results for Anbar and Nineveh: Is Iraq Headed for Complete Disintegration?" June 27, 2013.

[29] Prime Minister Maliki address at the U.S. Institute of Peace. Attended by the author, October 31, 2013.

[30] Kirk Sowell. "Sunni Voters and Iraq's Provincial Elections." July 12, 2013.

[31] Loveday Morris. "Iraqi Army Struggles in Battles Against Islamist Fighters in Anbar Province." Washington Post, February 27, 2014.

[32] Loveday Morris and Anne Gearan. "Kerry Says U.S. Will Help Iraq Against al-Qaeda but Won't Send Troops Back In." *Washington Post*, January 5, 2014.

[33] "U.S. Seeks to Resume Training of Iraqi Commandos." Dow Jones Newswire, January 9, 2014; Statement of Deputy Assistant Secretary of State Brett McGurk before the House Foreign Affairs Committee. February 5, 2014.

[34] http://www.state.gov/j/drl/rls/hrrpt/humanrightsreport/index.htm?year=2013&dlid=220355#wrapper

[35] Human Rights Watch. "Iraq's Information Crimes Law: Badly Written Provisions and Draconian Punishments Violate due Process and Free Speech." July 12, 2012.

[36] http://www.state.gov/j/drl/rls/irf/religiousfreedom/index.htm?year=2012&dlid=208390#wrapper

Iraq: Politics, Governance, and Human Rights   63

[37] Tim Arango. "Iraq Election Official's Arrest Casts Doubt on Prospects for Fair Voting." *New York Times*, April 17, 2012.

[38] Kristina Wong, "Iraq Resists U.S. Prod, Lets Iran Fly Arms to Syria." *Washington Times*, March 16, 2012.

[39] Sahar Issa. "Iraq Violence Dips Amid Rise in Syria." *Philadelphia Inquirer*, February 21, 2012.

[40] "Iraq General Says Forces Not Ready 'Until 2020.'" Agence France Presse, October 30, 2011.

[41] Prashant Rao. "Maliki Tells US' Boehner Iraqi Troops Are Ready." *Agence France Presse*, April 16, 2011.

[42] Aaron Davis. "Maliki Seeking Consensus on Troops." *Washington Post*, May 12, 2011.

[43] Author conversations with Iraq experts in Washington, DC, 2011.

[44] Eric Schmitt and Steven Lee Myers. "Plan Would Keep Military in Iraq Beyond Deadline." September 7, 2011.

[45] Iraq Signs Arms Deals Worth $4.2 Billion. *Washington Post*, October 10, 2012; Tony Capaccio. "Iraq Seeks Up to 30 General Dynamics Stryker Vehicles." Bloomberg News, November 19, 2012.

[46] John Hudson. "Iraqi Ambassador: Give Us Bigger Guns, And Then We'll Help on Syria." July 17, 2013.

[47] http://www.defensenews.com/article/20140106/DEFREG02/301060019/US-Speeds-Up-Drone-Missile-Deliveries-Aid-Iraq

[48] Adam Schreck. "Iraq Presses US For Faster Arms Deliveries." Yahoo.com, October 18, 2012.

[49] Defense News. December 12, 2013.

[50] Tim Arango. "U.S. May Scrap Costly Efforts to Train Iraqi Policy." *New York Times*, May 13, 2012.

[51] "U.S. Hopes For Stronger Military Ties With Iraq: General" Agence France-Presse, August 19, 2012.

[52] Dan De Luce. "U.S. 'Significant' in Iraq Despite Troop Exit: Dempsey." Agence France-Presse, August 21, 2012.

[53] Tim Arango. "Syrian Civil War Poses New Peril For Fragile Iraq." New York Times, September 25, 2012.

[54] Adam Entous et al. "CIA Ramps Up Role in Iraq." *Wall Street Journal*, March 12, 2013.

[55] Michael Gordon and Eric Schmitt. "As Security Deteriorates at Home, Iraqi Leader Arrives in U.S. Seeking Aid." *New York Times*, November 1, 2013.

[56] Author conversations with congressional staff and outside experts. October 2013.

[57] Remarks by the President on Ending the War in Iraq." http://www.whitehouse.gov, October 21, 2011.

[58] Ernesto Londono. "U.S. Clout Wanes in Iraq." *Washington Post*, March 24, 2013.

[59] Tim Arango. "U.S. Plans to Cut Its Staff by Half at Iraq Embassy." *New York Times*, February 8, 2012.

In: Internal Conflict Regions in the Middle East   ISBN: 978-1-63321-259-6
Editor: Dana V. Gray   © 2014 Nova Science Publishers, Inc.

Chapter 2

ARMED CONFLICT IN SYRIA: OVERVIEW AND U.S. RESPONSE[*]

Christopher M. Blanchard, Carla E. Humud and Mary Beth D. Nikitin

SUMMARY

Fighting continues across Syria, pitting government forces and their foreign allies against a range of anti-government insurgents, some of whom also are fighting amongst themselves. Since March 2011, the conflict has driven more than 2.6 million Syrians into neighboring countries as refugees (out of a total population of more than 22 million). Millions more Syrians are internally displaced and in need of humanitarian assistance, of which the United States remains the largest bilateral provider, with more than $1.7 billion in funding identified to date. U.S. nonlethal assistance to opposition forces was placed on hold in December 2013, as fighting in northern Syria disrupted mechanisms put in place to monitor and secure U.S. supplies. Administration officials have since resumed some assistance to select opposition groups.

---

[*] This is an edited, reformatted and augmented version of a Congressional Research Service publication RL33487, prepared for Members and Committees of Congress dated April 9, 2014.

Neither pro-Asad forces nor their opponents appear capable of consolidating their battlefield gains in Syria or achieving outright victory there in the short term. Improved coordination among some anti-government forces and attrition in government ranks make a swift reassertion of state control over all of Syria unlikely. Conflict between the Islamic State of Iraq and the Levant (ISIL, a.k.a. ISIS) and other anti-Asad forces has intensified. The war in Syria is exacerbating local sectarian and political conflicts within Lebanon and Iraq, threatening national stability.

In spite of an apparent shared antipathy toward ISIL's brutality among opposition groups, many anti-Asad armed forces and their activist counterparts remain divided over tactics, strategy, and their long-term political goals for Syria. As of March 2014, the most powerful and numerous anti-Asad armed forces seek outcomes that are contrary in significant ways to stated U.S. preferences for Syria's political future. Islamist militias seeking to impose varying degrees of Sunni Islamic law on Syrian society, including members of the Islamic Front, ISIL, and Jabhat al Nusra, have marginalized others who had received U.S. assistance.

The United States and other members of the United Nations Security Council seek continued Syrian government cooperation with efforts to remove chemical weapons from Syria and provide relief. The Security Council also has endorsed principles for a negotiated settlement of the conflict that could leave members of the current Syrian government in power as members of a transitional governing body, an outcome that some opposition groups reject. The FY2014 Consolidated Appropriations Act (H.R. 3547, P.L. 113-76) authorizes the Administration to provide nonlethal assistance in Syria for certain purposes notwithstanding other provisions of law that had restricted such assistance previously. The Administration is seeking $1.25 billion in State Department administered funding for the Syria crisis in FY2015, including $1.1 billion for humanitarian programs.

The humanitarian and regional security crises emanating from Syria now appear to be beyond the power of any single actor, including the United States, to contain or fully address. Large numbers of Syrian refugees, the growth of powerful armed extremist groups in Syria, and the assertive involvement of Iran, Turkey, and Sunni Arab governments in Syria's civil war are all negatively affecting the regional security environment in the Middle East. In light of these conditions and trends, Congress is likely to face choices about the investment of U.S. relief and security assistance funding in relation to the crisis in Syria and its effects on the region for years to come.

OVERVIEW

Fighting continues across Syria, pitting government forces and their foreign allies against a range of anti-government insurgents, some of whom also are fighting amongst themselves. Government forces are fighting on multiple fronts and have lost or ceded control of large areas of the country since 2011, but hold most major cities. The Asad government continues to receive support from Russia and Iran, and, contrary to some observers' predictions, has shown no indication of an imminent collapse. Opposition forces are formidable but lack unity of purpose, unity of command, and unified international support. Various opposition groups have, depending on the circumstances, cooperated and competed. At present, significant elements of the opposition are engaged in outright conflict against one another. Some observers suggest that more than 75% of the armed opposition may seek to replace the Asad government with a state ruled according to some form of Sunni Islamic law,[1] which non-Sunni minority groups oppose. Kurdish groups control areas of northeastern Syria and may seek autonomy or independence in the future.

Meanwhile, chemical weapons inspectors work to oversee and implement the terms of the September 2013 chemical disarmament agreement endorsed by the United Nations (U.N.) Security Council in Resolution 2118. Some rebel groups and regional governments have criticized the U.S. decision to forego a threatened military strike against Syrian government forces in response to the Syrian military's alleged use of chemical weapons in August. Members of Congress expressed a broad range of views regarding the potential use of force in Syria during intense debate in September, and Obama Administration officials have stated that they believe that the threat of the use of force by the United States was instrumental in convincing Syrian President Bashar al Asad to commit to the disarmament plan.

With internationally supervised disarmament proceeding, U.S. diplomatic efforts seek to shape the terms and conditions for negotiation to end the fighting and establish a transitional governing body as called for by a communiqué agreed to in Geneva in June 2012. That communiqué was further endorsed in Resolutions 2118 and 2139, and served as the basis for the January-February 2014 "Geneva II" talks in Switzerland involving some members of the Syrian opposition, representatives of the Syrian government, and delegates from dozens of countries. Those talks failed to address the establishment of a transitional body, based largely on Syrian government insistence that terrorism concerns be resolved first. Several unarmed and armed groups rejected the Geneva II talks outright, and opposition forces remain divided over questions of whether and under what conditions to participate in negotiations with the Asad government.

Inside Syria, neither pro-Asad forces nor their opponents appear capable of consolidating their battlefield gains or achieving outright victory in the short term. In February 2014, the U.S. intelligence community reported to Congress that a stalemate prevails in Syria, and that "decisively altering the course of the conflict in the next six months will prove difficult for either side." According to Director of National Intelligence James Clapper, the Syrian government and its allies have gained some ground in recent months. However, improved coordination among some anti-government forces and attrition in government ranks makes a swift reassertion of state control across all of Syria improbable.

THE GENEVA II TALKS

The January-February 2014 Geneva II talks brought many of the internal and external fault lines in the conflict into sharp relief. Divergent perspectives among Syrian parties to the conflict were reflected among their respective international backers. The negotiations failed to make progress toward the establishment of a transitional governing body (TGB), but provided an opportunity for some members of the U.S.-recognized National Coalition of Syrian Revolution and Opposition Forces (or Syrian Opposition Coalition, SOC) to demonstrate their capability to represent the interests of Syrians and potentially improve their standing with some of the disparate opposition forces engaged in fighting inside Syria. Nevertheless, other opposition groups, including several powerful Islamist militias, rejected the negotiations and stated their intention to keep fighting until their demands are met.

According to U.N. officials, the Syrian government delegation refused to engage in discussions aimed at establishing a TGB and sought to focus on the question of combatting terrorism. Syrian military operations, including attacks on rebel held areas of Aleppo using barrel bombs and other indiscriminate means, continued during the talks and killed hundreds of civilians. Prior to the talks, President Asad stated that the government had already laid out its peace initiative in January 2013.[2]

Under the first stage of this plan, the Syrian armed forces would halt military operations as soon as regional countries stopped funding and arming the opposition and when the opposition itself ceased attacks against the government.[3]

The United States and other members of the Core Group have reiterated their support for negotiations on the terms of the Geneva communiqué, while criticizing the Asad government for "obstruction" and praising the SOC delegation for its participation in the talks.[4] Syrian government representatives criticized what they viewed as the opposition delegation's unwillingness to fully discuss terrorism and its inability to make firm commitments on the actions of armed groups.[5] The Asad government appears unwilling to open discussions regarding any transitional arrangements until its concerns with regard to terrorism and anti-state violence are addressed. Opposition representatives acknowledge the threats posed by extremist groups, but view the establishment of transitional arrangements as necessary for undermining the legitimacy of violent extremist groups.

The potential for future talks is uncertain, although participants and international supporters on both sides characterized the end of the January-February round of discussions as a recess and agreed to a four point agenda to guide talks if they resume. The four agenda items, as described by Joint Special Representative for Syria (JSRS) Lakhdar Brahimi, are (1) violence and terrorism; (2) the TGB; (3) national institutions; and (4) national reconciliation and debate.[6] On February 16, Brahimi said, "it's not good for Syria that we come back for another round and fall in the same trap that we have been struggling with this week and most of the first round. So I think it is better that every side goes back and reflect and take their responsibility: do they want this process to take place or not?"

Obama Administration officials have reiterated their shared view that once a Transitional Governing Body [TGB] called for by the Geneva communiqué is established by mutual consent and has full control over state security services, "Asad and his close associates with blood on their hands will have no role in Syria." Speaking in Montreux, Switzerland on January 22, Secretary of State Kerry said that an emphasis on mutual consent would necessarily preclude Asad from participation in a transitional government, along with "those who have supported him" and "thousands of violent extremists" currently fighting the Asad government.[7]

> Russian officials have called on the United States and others not to prejudge the outcome of talks to establish transitional governing arrangements, which many outside observers view as an indication that Russia does not view Asad's departure as a necessary condition for ending the conflict.
>
> United Nations Security Council Resolution 2139 reiterated the Council's endorsement of the Geneva communiqué and demanded that parties support its implementation "leading to a transition that meets the legitimate aspirations of the Syrian people and enables them independently and democratically to determine their own future."

Combat between Islamic State of Iraq and the Levant (ISIL, a.k.a. ISIS, **Figure 2)**[8] and other anti-Asad forces across northern Syria has intensified since late December 2013. In spite of an apparent shared antipathy among opposition groups toward ISIL's brutality, many anti-Asad armed forces and their activist counterparts remain divided over tactics, strategy, and their long-term political goals for Syria. U.S. intelligence estimates the strength of the insurgency in Syria at "somewhere between 75,000 or 80,000 or up to 110,000 to 115,000 insurgents, who are organized into more than 1,500 groups of widely varying political leanings."

As of March 2014, the most powerful and numerous anti-Asad armed forces seek outcomes that are contrary in significant ways to stated U.S. preferences for Syria's political future. Islamist militias seeking to enforce varying degrees of what they recognize as Sunni Islamic law in Syrian society—among them members of the Islamic Front (see below), ISIL, and Jabhat al Nusra— have marginalized other armed groups, including some that received U.S. assistance. U.S. intelligence community leaders have identified the approximately 26,000 members of ISIL, Jabhat al Nusra, and Ahrar al Sham (a key component of the Islamic Front) both as extremists and as the most effective opposition forces in the field. U.S. officials believe that as many as "7,500 foreign fighters from some 50 countries" have travelled to Syria, including Al Qaeda-linked veterans of previous conflicts and Western nationals.[9]

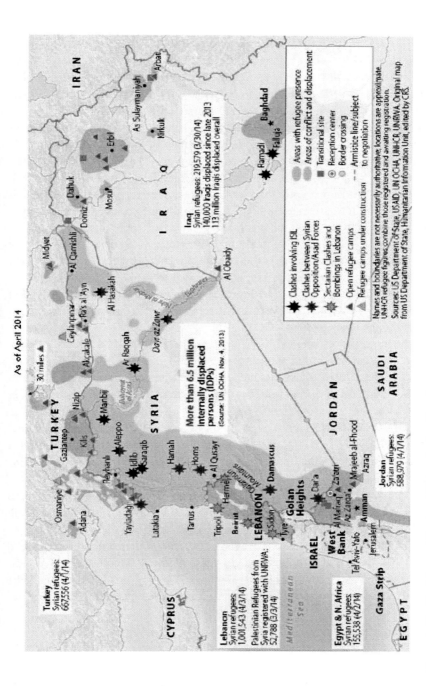

Figure 1. Conflict Map and Regional Humanitarian Situation.

In its recent threat assessment testimony, the U.S. intelligence community judged that Asad "remains unwilling to negotiate himself out of power" and "almost certainly intends to remain the ruler of Syria."[10] Iran and Hezbollah share that objective and continue to invest heavily in Syria on Asad's behalf. That testimony noted that infighting among anti-Asad groups has given government forces and their supporters an advantage in some areas, but that an overall stalemate is likely to prevail in the conflict for the foreseeable future.[11]

As clashes and diplomatic discussions continue, Syrian civilians continue to suffer in what U.S. Director of National Intelligence James Clapper has described as an "apocalyptic disaster." U.N. sources report that since March 2011, the conflict has driven more than 2.6 million Syrians into neighboring countries as refugees (out of a total population of more than 22 million). According to U.S. officials, more than 6.5 million Syrians are internally displaced. The United States is the largest bilateral provider of humanitarian assistance, with more than $1.7 billion allocated to date.[12] In December 2013, the U.N. Office for the Coordination of Humanitarian Assistance (UNOCHA) appealed for an additional $6.5 billion in humanitarian assistance funding to respond to the crisis in 2014.[13]

The negative effects of the humanitarian and regional security crises emanating from Syria now appear to be beyond the power of any single actor, including the United States, to independently contain or fully address. The region-wide flood of Syrian refugees, the growth of armed extremist groups in Syria, and the assertive involvement of Iran, Turkey, and Sunni Arab governments in Syria's civil war are negatively affecting overall regional stability. The war in Syria also is exacerbating local sectarian and political conflicts within Lebanon and Iraq, where violence is escalating and threatens national stability.

Policy makers in the United States and other countries appear to feel both compelled to respond to these crises and hesitant to embrace options for doing so that may have political and security risks such as the commitment of military forces to combat or the provision of large-scale material assistance to armed elements of the opposition. In light of these conditions and trends, Congress may face tough choices about U.S. policy toward Syria and the related expenditure of U.S. relief and security assistance funds for years to come.

ANTI-ASAD FORCES

Anti-Asad forces have been engaged in a series of realignments and internal conflicts since mid-2013, creating complications for external parties seeking to provide support. To date, the United States has sought to build the capacity of the Syrian Opposition Coalition (SOC) and local activists as well as to provide nonlethal and lethal support to armed groups affiliated with a Supreme Military Command Council (SMC), whose leadership is in flux. In mid-February, SOC figures announced that General Salim Idris was being replaced as SMC commander by Brigadier General Abdul-Ilah al Bashir al Noemi: Idris and other commanders have rejected the change and attempts to resolve differences continue. Many armed Sunni groups disavowed the SOC's participation in January-February 2014 talks with the Asad government in Switzerland. The U.S. government has recognized the SOC as the legitimate representative of the Syrian opposition.

In late 2013, a number of powerful Islamist militia groups—some of which formerly recognized the leadership of Idris and the SMC—announced the formation of a new Islamic Front.[14] The Islamic Front and other recently created opposition coalitions active in northern Syria, such as the Syrian Revolutionaries Front (SRF) and the Mujahedin Army, have been engaged in a campaign to evict ISIL from areas of northern and eastern Syria since early January 2014. Prior to the outbreak of the confrontation with ISIL, many expert observers considered the Front to be the most powerful element of the armed opposition in northern Syria (see the **Appendix**). The pressures of confrontation between members of the Islamic Front and ISIL may be undermining the cohesion of the group, as differences in ideology, strategy, priorities, and preferred tactics encourage individuals, units, and groups within the Front to reconsider their positions.

The Front's charter declared its goals to include "the full overthrow of the Al Asad regime in Syria and for building an Islamic state ruled by the sharia of God Almighty alone."[15] The Front explicitly rejects the concepts of secularism and a civil state, rejects "foreign dictates," and is committed to maintaining the territorial integrity of Syria. Front leaders have rejected the SOC and issued a statement on January 20 in conjunction with the Mujahedin Army and another group rejecting the Geneva II talks and setting a series of conditions that must be achieved before they will contemplate a settlement.[16] The statement calls for "the entire regime, including its head and all its criminal figures" to step down and calls for security bodies to be held legally accountable. The Front and its allies further demand that there be "no interference in the form of the future state after the regime [steps down] and no imposition of any matter that conflicts with the Islamic identity of the masses or which takes away the rights of any section of society."

Jabhat al Nusra, an Al Qaeda-affiliated militia and U.S.-designated Foreign Terrorist Organization, first sought to mediate between ISIL and its adversaries but has since engaged in battles with ISIL and called on ISIL members to defect to other Islamist groups in light of ISIL's intransigent brutality (**Figure 2**). In general, Al Nusra is viewed as more accommodating and cooperative than ISIL by other opposition forces, including some who oppose its ideology. Some members of the Islamic Front and other non-Islamist opposition groups appear to coordinate operations with Jabhat al Nusra in different parts of the country.

The ISIL-opposition battles have momentarily supplanted deeper questions about the future composition and direction of the Syrian opposition and the provision of external support to its armed elements. The formation of the Islamic Front in November 2013 raised questions about which forces actually remained affiliated with the SMC and whether they are credible partners for the United States and others. Then, in December, Islamic Front fighters took control of facilities and equipment belonging to the U.S.-backed SMC, including some U.S.-supplied materiel. The incident, the Front's continued rejection of the U.S.-preferred strategy of negotiation, and the group's long-term goal of establishing an Islamic state in Syria raise fundamental questions about whether and how the United States should engage with the Front and its allies, despite their capabilities and prominence.

In a January 2014 communiqué from their meeting in Paris, the United States and other members of the "Friends of Syria core group of countries" [AKA the "London 11" or "Core Group"][17] stated that, "all armed groups must respect democratic and pluralistic values, recognize the political authority of the National Coalition [SOC] and accept the prospect of a democratic transition negotiated in Geneva...."[18] It remains to be seen whether statements by the Islamic Front and others rejecting secular democracy, the political authority of the SOC, and negotiations with the Asad government will preclude engagement by outsiders with the Front and its allies against Al Qaeda-affiliated groups in Syria or against pro-Asad forces.

TERRORIST THREATS POSED BY SYRIA- AND IRAQ-BASED SUNNI EXTREMISTS

Since January 2014, U.S. officials have made several public statements describing the potential for Syria-based extremists to pose a direct terrorist threat to the United States. U.S. and European officials have highlighted the particular threat posed by foreign fighters, some of whom hold U.S. and European passports. Central Intelligence Agency Director John Brennan said in testimony before the House Permanent Select Committee on Intelligence in February 2014 that:

> ...there are three groups of people that are a concern, from an extremist standpoint; Ahrar al Sham, Jabhat al Nusra, which is the Al Qaeda element within Syria, and the Islamic State of Iraq and the Levant (ISIL). It's those latter two I think are most dedicated to the terrorist agenda. We are concerned about the use of Syrian territory by the Al Qaeda organization to recruit individuals and develop the capability to be able not just to carry out attacks inside of Syria, but also to use Syria as a launching pad. So it's those elements—Al Qaeda and ISIL - that I'm concerned about, especially the ability of these groups to attract individuals from other countries, both from the West, as well as throughout the Middle East and South Asia, and with some experienced operatives there who have had experience in carrying out a global jihad. ...There are camps inside of both Iraq and Syria that are used by Al Qaeda to develop capabilities that are applicable, both in the theater, as well as beyond.[19]

Brennan called the threat posed by these groups "a near-term concern, as well as a long-term concern," and said that "the intelligence community, including CIA, is working very closely with our partners internationally to try to address the terrorist challenge." In press reports, unnamed intelligence officials have described the foreign fighter problem as "one of the most significant threats we're dealing with," and the Federal Bureau of Investigation reportedly is monitoring several returnees from Syria. Homeland Security Secretary Jeh Johnson has called the terrorist threat from Syria "a matter of homeland security."

Secretary Kerry has accused the Asad government of "funding some of those extremists—even purposely ceding some territory to them in order to make them more of a problem so he can make the argument that he is somehow the protector against them."[20]

> Several press reports allege that opposition groups have sold oil and petroleum products from areas under their control to agents of the Syrian government. The Asad government's past permissiveness toward anti-U.S. Sunni extremist groups during the U.S. presence in Iraq and Asad's release of several prominent extremists from prison in 2011 raise further questions about the regime's strategy.
>
> In July 2012, ISIL leader Abu Bakr al Baghdadi warned U.S. leaders that "The mujahidin have set out to chase the affiliates of your armies that have fled. ...You will see them in your own country, God willing. The war with you has just begun."[21] In January 2014, Baghdadi concluded a statement on recent regional developments with a further warning for the United States: "Know, O defender of the Cross, that a proxy war will not help you in the Levant, just as it will not help you in Iraq. Soon, you will be in direct conflict—God permitting—against your will. The youths of Islam have steeled themselves for this day. 'So wait; we too will wait with you," [partial Koranic verse, Al Tawbah, 9:52].'"[22]

Some reports suggest the Syrian Revolutionaries Front (SRF) and one of its prominent commanders, Jamal Maarouf, or individual elements of the SMC may emerge as focal points for new external assistance from the United States and others seeking to back relatively moderate armed opposition forces. However, some Syrians consider members of the SRF and similar locally organized forces to be corrupt, and the provision of outside assistance to select groups on conditional political terms may provoke divisions and further infighting. In particular, Islamist forces may seek to delegitimize and militarily target other groups perceived to be cooperating with the United States and other outside powers. Reconciling U.S. and other third party support for armed opposition groups with U.S. diplomatic efforts seeking a negotiated settlement and a transitional governing body may be challenged by the refusal of certain armed groups to endorse the terms of proposed settlements.

PRO-ASAD FORCES[23]

The Syrian government has continued military and security operations against insurgents while pursuing political measures intended to boost Asad's domestic and international legitimacy. Government forces in March continued operations in Aleppo and areas north of Damascus, in an effort to isolate rebels and sever their supply lines.[24] Meanwhile, Syria's Information Minister in

Armed Conflict in Syria: Overview and U.S. Response

mid-March stated that presidential elections would be held in the summer of 2014 in all provinces except Raqqah, which is under the control of ISIL.[25]

Asad is planning to stand for reelection, according to U.S. and Syrian officials,[26] despite opposition demands that he cede power to a transitional governing body as outlined in the June 2012 Geneva communiqué. Asad has stated that presidential elections will include multiple candidates in accordance with Syria's new constitution, which was approved by referendum in 2012.[27] However, the new election law stipulates that candidates must have maintained continuous residence in Syria for 10 years prior to nomination and must hold no other nationality or prior criminal convictions[28]—effectively disqualifying many members of the Syrian Opposition Council who currently reside in exile. The United States and other members of the Core Group on Syria have rejected Asad's potential candidacy. On April 3, the Core Group issued a statement saying:

> any unilateral decision by the Syrian regime to hold presidential elections would be entirely inconsistent with the Geneva Communique's call for the establishment of a transitional governing body to oversee constitutional reforms leading to free and fair elections in a neutral environment. Elections organized by the Assad regime would be a parody of democracy, would reveal the regime's rejection of the basis of the Geneva talks, and would deepen the division of Syria.[29]

As described above, the Syrian government participated in the Geneva II negotiations, but insisted that counterterrorism issues be addressed before any discussion of a potential transition. At present, Asad appears disinclined to make concessions that would significantly undermine his hold on power, particularly if he assesses that his military ultimately can prevail over insurgents or at least hold them at bay. Asad may judge that his move to declare and destroy his government's chemical weapons has eased international pressure on his government, and that peace talks will further expose opposition divisions—perhaps thereby demonstrating that his government lacks a credible negotiating partner.

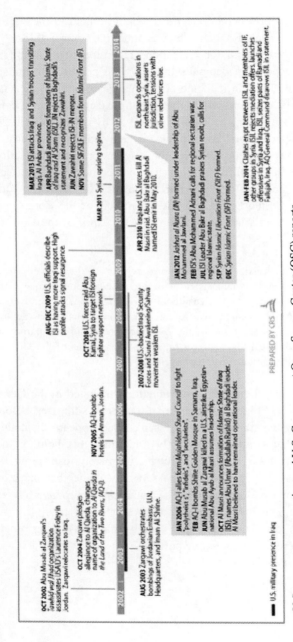

Source: U.S. government reporting and U.S. Government Open Source Center (OSC) reports.

Figure 2. Evolution of Al Qaeda Affiliates and Select Extremist Forces in Iraq and Syria, 2002-2014.

Armed Conflict in Syria: Overview and U.S. Response

Shia Armed Groups and Iranian Support for the Syrian Government

The involvement of Shia militias and Iran in the Syrian conflict has evolved since 2011 from an advisory to an operational role, with forces in some cases now fighting alongside Syrian troops. Lebanese Hezbollah and Iran have traditionally depended on the presence of a friendly government in Damascus to facilitate the transit of weapons from Iran to Hezbollah and to preserve their ability to challenge Israel. Hezbollah and Iranian roles in Syria appear designed to bolster Asad's ability to suppress the opposition but also to secure their interests in Syria in the event that the Asad government does not survive.[30]

Hezbollah

In August 2012, the U.S. Treasury Department sanctioned Hezbollah for providing training, advice, and logistical support to the Syrian government.[31] U.S. officials also noted that Hezbollah has helped the Syrian government push rebel forces out of some areas in Syria. Hezbollah Secretary General Hassan Nasrallah, who was personally sanctioned for his role in overseeing Hezbollah's assistance to Damascus, publicly acknowledged Hezbollah's involvement in Syria in May 2013. Nasrallah also recently expressed confidence that the risk of the Asad regime's defeat and the partition of Syria had passed even if a war of attrition may persist.[32] He further referred to the need for reconciliation initiatives to bolster the Asad government's support among Syrians.

As of March 2014, Hezbollah fighters remained active in the Qalamoun region northwest of Damascus, where they reportedly assisted in the recent recapture of the opposition stronghold of Yabroud.[33] A senior Israeli military official in March 2014 stated that Hezbollah currently maintains 4,000 to 5,000 fighters in Syria.[34]

Over the past year, Hezbollah has worked with the Syrian military to protect regime supply lines by helping to clear rebel-held towns along the Damascus-Homs stretch of the M-5 highway.[35] Hezbollah personnel in 2013 played significant roles in battles around Al Qusayr and the Qalamoun Mountains region, in which rebel presence along the highway threatened the government's ability to move forces and to access predominantly Alawite strongholds on the coast.[36] Hezbollah forces on the Lebanese side of the border reportedly monitor and target rebel positions near the border that facilitate attacks in Syria and Lebanon.

80   Christopher M. Blanchard, Carla E. Humud and Mary Beth D. Nikitin

Last year saw an uptick in violence against Hezbollah targets in Lebanon, and the militia's support for the Asad government appears to be contributing to the rise in sectarian violence and tension in Lebanon. Jabhat al Nusra and ISIL have claimed responsibility for attacks on Hezbollah-controlled areas of Beirut and eastern Lebanon, describing the attacks as retaliation for Hezbollah's intervention in Syria.[37]

Iraqi Militias

Analysts estimate that there are between 2,000 and 5,000 Iraqi Shia fighting in Syria on behalf of the Syrian government.[38] Many hail from Iraqi Shia political and militia groups including Asa'ib Ahl al Haq and Kata'ib Hezbollah. Members identify their objective as the defense of Shia holy sites such as the tomb of Sayyida Zeinab, the granddaughter of the Prophet Mohammad, in southern Damascus. Other reports describe these groups as assuming a broad operational role, noting that militias have formed sniper teams, led ambushes, established checkpoints, and provided infantry support for Syrian armored units.[39]

It is difficult to assess the motivations of individual Iraqi fighters in Syria or determine whether Asad's survival is their primary goal. Some of the fighters appear to be young volunteers driven by a desire to protect Shia holy sites, while others are trained militiamen who previously fought coalition forces in Iraq. Reports suggest that Iraqi fighters receive training in Iran before being flown in small batches into Syria, and that they work closely with Lebanese Hezbollah.[40] However, it is unclear who ultimately exercises command and control over these militias. Clashes between Iraqi and local Syrian militias in mid-2013 resulted in some Iraqi combatants refusing to fight under Syrian command.[41] Recent attacks by ISIL and others on Iraqi Shia could prompt some of these groups to redirect their efforts to domestic struggles.

Iranian Support

Since 2011, Iran has provided technical, training, and financial assistance both to the Syrian government and to pro-regime Shia militias operating in Syria. In February 2012, the U.S. Treasury Department sanctioned the Iranian Ministry of Intelligence and Security (MOIS) for providing substantial technical assistance to Syrian intelligence, noting that MOIS also participated in multiple joint projects with Hezbollah.[42] Treasury also designated the Islamic Revolutionary Guard Corps-Quds Force (IRGC-QF) for training Syrian forces, and Iraqi Shia militias fighting in Syria have credited Iran for providing training and coordinating their travel into the country. Mohammad Ali Jafari, head of the IRGC, acknowledged in September 2012 that some members of the Quds Force were present in Syria,[43] and U.S. officials have described them as also working closely with Hezbollah. Regional observers in March 2014 estimated that between 1,000 and 1,500 IRGC members were present in Syria.[44] In terms of non-lethal aid, Iran has provided Syria with billions of dollars in credit to purchase oil, food, and import goods from Iran.[45]

CHEMICAL WEAPONS AND DISARMAMENT: BACKGROUND[46]

A major policy concern of the United States has been the use or loss of control of chemical weapons stocks in Syria during that country's ongoing civil war. The United States and other countries have assessed that the Syrian government has used chemical weapons repeatedly against opposition forces and civilians in the country. The largest-scale use to date was reportedly on August 21, 2013. The U.N. Mission to Investigate Allegations of the Use of Chemical Weapons in the Syrian Arab Republic released its report on September 16, 2013, concluding that surface-to-surface rockets containing sarin were used in the Ghouta area of Damascus against civilians on a "relatively large scale." The U.N. investigative mission was not tasked with assigning culpability for the attacks.

The Obama Administration threatened military action against Syria in response to chemical weapons use in Syria in August 2013. In a diplomatic solution that resulted in the Administration withdrawing the threat, Syria agreed to join the international Chemical Weapons Convention (CWC), which requires Syria to destroy all of its chemical weapons stocks and production facilities. Based on a joint U.S.-Russian proposal, the Executive Council of the Organization for the Prohibition of Chemical Weapons (OPCW), an intergovernmental body tasked with implementation of the CWC, approved a destruction plan under which Syria is required to destroy all chemical weapons by June 30, 2014. Under Security Council Resolution 2118, the OPCW is to report to the U.N. Security Council on implementation on a monthly basis.

Syria is required to declare and destroy all of its chemical weapons stocks and production facilities under international supervision. Syria is believed to have more than 1,000 metric tons of chemical warfare agents and precursor chemicals. This stockpile includes several hundred metric tons of the nerve

82   Christopher M. Blanchard, Carla E. Humud and Mary Beth D. Nikitin

agent sarin, which represents the bulk of Syria's chemical weapons stockpile. Damascus also has several hundred metric tons of mustard agent in ready-to-use form and several metric tons of the nerve agent VX.

A joint mission of U.N. and OPCW personnel was created to monitor and facilitate Syrian chemical weapons disarmament.[47] OPCW-U.N. experts arrived in Damascus on October 1, 2013, and began to inspect Syria's declared chemical weapons facilities. The OPCW spokesman told reporters on October 31 that the Syrian government met the November 1, 2013, destruction deadline for disabling production equipment, and that all chemical weapons stocks and agents in Syria were under "tamper-proof" seal. The first stage of destruction activities focused on destroying "critical equipment" at chemical weapons production facilities and mixing and filling units.

Removal of Chemicals

The current stage of the chemical weapons destruction process involves transportation and removal of chemical weapons agents from the country. These are liquid chemicals that have not been loaded into delivery vehicles. The OPCW Executive Council on November 14, 2013, approved the destruction of Syria's chemical weapons agents ("priority 1" chemicals) outside of Syria due to the security situation in the country. The United States and others have provided equipment to the OPCW-U.N. Joint Mission to help safely transfer these chemicals from storage facilities to the Syrian port of Latakia. Once all the chemicals are at the port, Danish and Norwegian ships are to pick up the chemicals and remove them from Syria. The first quantity of priority chemicals was moved to the port of Latakia in early January 2014.

No country had agreed to conduct destruction operations on its territory due to public concerns about the dangers of the material, but also due to the short timeline for destruction which in some cases would not have allowed for the required environmental and health impact assessments. Therefore, the United States plans to neutralize the liquid chemical weapons agents on board the Maritime Administration's Motor Vessel (MV) *Cape Ray* using newly installed field deployable hydrolysis systems (FDHS). This ship is expected to receive 700 metric tons of both mustard agent and DF compound, a key component in sarin.[48] U.S. personnel, including 64 Army chemical specialists, will run the operation. The MV *Cape Ray* is now at the port of Rota, Spain. Once removed from Latakia, the most dangerous compounds in approximately 60 containers will be transferred to the *Cape Ray* at the Italian port of Gioia

Armed Conflict in Syria: Overview and U.S. Response 83

Tauro for destruction at sea in international waters. NATO has canceled cooperation with the Russian Federation on guarding the *Cape Ray* during chemical weapons destruction activities because of Russia's actions in Ukraine.[49] Less sensitive chemicals will be shipped to commercial processing facilities, for example in the United Kingdom. Companies in Finland and the United States were awarded contracts for processing the liquid waste from the destruction process.[50]

Syria did not meet the original deadline of December 31, 2013, for removal of these agents from its territory. According to the OPCW Director General, the delays were caused by "security concerns, the procurement and delivery of large quantities of packaging and transportation materials and equipment, and adverse weather conditions."[51] Reports in early January quoted a Syrian government official as saying two CW storage sites have been under attack.[52] The Syrian government also missed a February 5, 2014, deadline, raising questions about the intentions of the Syrian government. Syria has asked for a new deadline of mid-May. In February, the U.N. Security Council called upon Syria to expedite removal of the chemicals. The United States in particular had been critical of the slow progress by the Syrian government. As U.S. Ambassador to the OPCW Robert Mikulak said,

> The international community has put into place everything that is necessary for transport and destruction of these chemicals. Sufficient equipment and material has been provided to Syria. The ships to carry the chemicals away from Syria are waiting. The U.S. ship to destroy CW agent and precursors is now in the region and waiting. Commercial facilities to destroy other chemicals have been selected and contracts awarded; they are waiting. And yet Syria continues to drag its feet.[53]

In March, OPCW-U.N. Joint Mission Special Coordinator Sigrid Kaag described "important progress" in efforts to expedite the transfer and destruction of chemicals and encouraged the Syrian government "to sustain the current pace."[54] As of April 8, Secretary Kerry confirmed the March 20 Joint Mission estimate that the Syrian government had moved eleven shipments of chemicals to the port of Latakia, representing around 53.6% of total stocks to be removed.[55] Secretary Kerry also reaffirmed that he has been working with the Russian government to expedite the transport of chemicals to Latakia for removal, so that the deadline for destruction of the chemicals could be met.

Destruction of Production Facilities

The Syrian government also did not meet the deadline of March 15, 2014, for destruction of its 12 chemical weapons production facilities, and has proposed that the facilities not be completely destroyed but instead made inaccessible.[56] The CWC requires that production facilities be "physically destroyed." U.S. Ambassador to the OPCW Robert Mikulak said in a February statement that the Executive Council should require Syria to physically destroy the facilities in line with the Convention.[57] The OPCW is now working on a destruction plan for these facilities with Syria.

Despite these delays, however, U.N. officials say they are optimistic that the final deadline, June 30, 2014, for destruction of all chemical weapons and production facilities will be met.

U.S. and International Funding for CW Elimination Efforts

The international community, including the United States, is contributing both technical and financial assistance to the OPCW-U.N. Joint Mission. In-kind technical assistance to date includes specialized packaging from the United States for transporting chemical weapons in Syria, security related support from Russia for Syrian ground movement of the materials, and cargo ships and naval vessels from Denmark and Norway.[58] Italy has volunteered to provide a port for transferring the agent from the cargo ships to the *Cape Ray*; the United Kingdom and Germany have provided a chemical processing facility for the destruction of some of the chemical materials.

According to the State Department, the United States has given approximately $6 million in financial assistance to the OPCW and U.N. joint mission through the State Department-administered Nonproliferation and Disarmament Fund. The United States has also given significant in-kind assistance to international inspectors. The largest contribution to the international effort has come from the Department of Defense Cooperative Threat Reduction (CTR) Program. On April 8, Deputy Assistant Secretary of Defense for Countering Weapons of Mass Destruction Rebecca K.C. Hersman said that the CTR program had allocated $160 million to support the CW elimination effort. DOD CTR also accepted $19 million in contributions from Germany, the UK, and Canada to assist with CTR programs, including the effort in Syria. Since the bulk of this funding was spent preparing the MV *Cape Ray* and equipping inspectors, the budget request for FY2015 is less than

Armed Conflict in Syria: Overview and U.S. Response

what was spent this past year—$15.7 million for technical expertise and resources to support the U.N.-OPCW Joint Mission in FY2015.

U.S. POLICY AND ASSISTANCE

Debates over U.S. policy toward Syria since 2011 have repeatedly returned to the question of U.S. military intervention, whether to protect civilians, target terrorist groups, or punish Syrian forces suspected of involvement in chemical weapons attacks or other attacks on opposition-held areas. To date, Administration officials have stated that U.S. military intervention to shape the outcome of Syria's civil conflict or to change the Syrian regime may not achieve U.S. objectives, and may lead to unintended negative consequences. Administration officials have cited a number of reasons for their reluctance to undertake direct military intervention or provide large-scale assistance to shift the balance of power in Syria, including fears of exacerbating the violence; inviting greater regional spillover or intervention; or opening a power vacuum that could benefit the extremists who are part of the opposition.[59] Uncertain costs, military constraints, and domestic political opposition to such involvement also are likely factors.

Some critics of the Administration's policy argue that many of these negative outcomes are occurring even in the absence of U.S. intervention and suggest that the image and influence of the United States are weakened by a refusal to intervene to protect civilians or respond to provocations. Others express concern that military intervention will exacerbate negative conditions prevailing on the ground and suggest that the United States cannot ensure that intervention or support provided to opposition groups will not benefit extremists. Recent Administration official statements concerning potential terrorist threats emanating from Syria have led to a reconsideration of many of these questions by some Members of Congress and the public. Some press reports suggest that Administration officials may be revisiting policy options that could expand U.S. involvement in the conflict in Syria, but U.S. officials have declined to confirm or deny reports about the contours of internal deliberations. On April 8, Secretary of State Kerry referred to ongoing consideration of policy options in testimony before the Senate Foreign Relations Committee and suggested that the United States was more engaged in supporting opposition elements than it had been to date.

While condemning Asad as a thug and a murderer and aiding some of his adversaries, Administration officials have continued to stress the need for a negotiated political solution to the conflict in the hopes of keeping the Syrian state intact, securing its weapon stockpiles and borders, and combating extremist groups now active there. The implementation of U.S. strategy in Syria to date has included the provision of both nonlethal and lethal assistance to select Syrian opposition groups, a sustained international diplomatic effort to establish a negotiated transition, and the provision of humanitarian assistance in Syria and neighboring countries. Through 2013, these initiatives were implemented under the auspices of an ad hoc series of assistance notifications to Congress providing for the waiver of certain restrictions on the use of U.S. funds for assistance in Syria and the assertion of emergency contingency authorities to reprogram and allocate funds for use in response to the crisis. Cumulatively, the notifications illustrate an evolution of U.S. involvement in the direction of seeking deeper partnership with select opposition actors on the ground in Syria, while seeking to bolster and unify opposition figures based outside of Syria.

At the October 2013 Friends of Syria conference in London, Secretary Kerry announced that the United States, along with other members of the "London 11" group, had "agreed to increase ... coordinated assistance to the opposition, including to the Syrian Opposition Coalition.... And we also committed to do more to assist the brave people who are on the ground in Syria." The Obama Administration subsequently notified Congress of plans to expand nonlethal assistance to various opposition groups. Through 2013, U.S. efforts to improve coordination among opposition groups in aid delivery had mixed success, with some observers criticizing the SOC's Assistance Coordination Unit (ACU) for lacking capacity and duplicating partnerships among donors and local organizations.

As of April 2014, the United States had allocated nearly $260 million in support of the non-armed opposition (including the SOC and local activists), more than half of which had been delivered as of late March.[60] The delivery of some assistance to select groups reportedly has been resumed after having been suspended as a result of the Islamic Front's seizure of SOC/SMC-controlled warehouse facilities and intra-opposition fighting in northern Syria.[61] The FY2014 Consolidated Appropriations bill (H.R. 3547, P.L. 113-76) provides new authority for the Administration to use FY2014 and previously appropriated monies in the Economic Support Fund (ESF) account to provide nonlethal assistance for certain purposes in Syria (see textbox below). An unspecified amount of funding may be subject to this authority.

Armed Conflict in Syria: Overview and U.S. Response

Table 1. U.S. Foreign Assistance for Syria,FY2013-FY2015 Request
(In current $ thousands, Fiscal Year denotes source of funds)

Account	FY2013 (Actual)	FY2014 (Estimate)	FY2015 (Request)
ESF	20,780 (OCO)	n.a.	125,000 (OCO)
INCLE	0	n.a.	10,000 (OCO)
NADR	0	n.a.	20,000
PKO	38,620 (OCO)	n.a.	0
FFP	18,338	n.a.	0
Total[a]	**77,738**	**n.a.**	**155,000**

Source: State Department and Foreign Operations and Related Programs, Congressional Budget Justification, FY2015.

Notes: FY2014 estimates for Syria spending were not available as of April 2014. Funds appropriated in fiscal years prior to FY2013 have supported U.S. assistance programs since 2011. n.a. = not available.

a. The FY2013 total figure does not reflect all of the $260 million allocated for support to the Syrian opposition to date. The FY2015 Syria request includes, but Table 3 does not show, $1.1 billion within Migration and Refugee Assistance (MRA-OCO) and International Disaster Assistance (IDA-OCO) accounts expected to be used for humanitarian assistance related to the Syria conflict.

FY2015 Budget Request for Syria

The FY2015 assistance request for Syria reflects the two main elements of the Obama Administration's policy response: (1) humanitarian assistance to meet the needs of internally displaced Syrians and refugees in neighboring countries, and (2) political, economic, and non-lethal military support for national and local opposition groups. Funds provided since 2011 in Syria and in neighboring countries for these combined purposes exceed $2 billion to date.

Of the total $1.26 billion in FY2015 funding requested specifically for Syria in the foreign operations budget request, $1.1 billion in Overseas Contingency Operations funds would support humanitarian response needs from the Migration and Refugee Assistance (MRA-OCO) and International Disaster Assistance (IDA-OCO) accounts. A further $155 million from the Economic Support Fund-Overseas Contingency Operations (ESF-OCO), International Narcotics Control and Law Enforcement-Overseas Contingency Operations (INCLE-OCO), and Nonproliferation, Anti-terrorism, De-mining, and Related Programs (NADR) accounts would support the Syrian opposition and transition related initiatives. If a transition should occur, FY2015 funds would support a political transition toward democracy, as well as reconstruction and recovery efforts. Specific proposals for the use of those funds have not been made available as of April 8, 2014.

Issues Shaping Future U.S. Assistance

As with humanitarian assistance, U.S. efforts to support local security and service delivery efforts to date have been hindered by a lack of regular access to areas in need. According to Administration officials, border closures, ongoing fighting, and risks from extremist groups have presented unique challenges. U.S. officials have stated their expectation that U.S. equipment will be returned to the control of SMC leaders by the Islamic Front and reiterated their view that the SOC and SMC remain the "legitimate representatives of the Syrian opposition and the Syrian people."[62] On January 12, the United States and other Core Group members stated that they "fully support the Supreme Military Council of the Free Syrian Army and other democratic opposition forces in their action against the Islamic State of Iraq and the Levant (ISIL)."

In light of these developments, the future nature and direction of U.S. engagement with certain Syrian opposition groups may be in flux. On the one hand, advocates of continued U.S. support for opposition groups aligned with U.S. values and preferences argue that the withdrawal or reduction of such assistance would bolster less cooperative or friendly groups. Advocates further argue that if the United States withdraws or reduces its support, then it may "force" moderate groups to turn to extremist groups for funding and support— thereby increasing the influence of extremists while reducing U.S. leverage. On the other hand, critics of continued U.S. support argue that such assistance risks exacerbating rivalry among opposition groups and reducing the credibility of groups and individuals seen to be aligned with the United States. Critics of support further point to problems in ensuring the identity of end users of provided support and the uses of U.S.-provided support. Administration officials have stated that they remain open to engagement with all opposition groups not affiliated with Al Qaeda. The Islamic Front reportedly has rebuffed U.S. requests for consultation to date, and its charter states that it rejects "foreign dictates that undermine its decision-making capabilities."[63]

FY2014 CONSOLIDATED APPROPRIATIONS ACT AND NONLETHAL ASSISTANCE IN SYRIA

Section 7041(i) of Division K of the FY2014 Consolidated Appropriations Act (H.R. 3547, P.L. 113-76) significantly expands the Administration's authority to provide nonlethal assistance in Syria for certain purposes using the Economic Support Fund (ESF) account. Such assistance had been restricted by a series of preexisting provisions of law (including some terrorism-related provisions) that required the President to assert emergency and contingency authorities to provide such assistance to the Syrian opposition and communities in Syria. The new authority makes FY2014 and prior year ESF funding available "notwithstanding any other provision of law for non-lethal assistance for programs to address the needs of civilians affected by conflict in Syria, and for programs that seek to—

(A) establish governance in Syria that is representative, inclusive, and accountable;

(B) develop and implement political processes that are democratic, transparent, and adhere to the rule of law;

(C) further the legitimacy of the Syrian opposition through cross-border programs;

(D) develop civil society and an independent media in Syria;

(E) promote economic development in Syria;

(F) document, investigate, and prosecute human rights violations in Syria, including through transitional justice programs and support for nongovernmental organizations; and

(G) counter extremist ideologies."

The act requires the Secretary of State to "take all appropriate steps to ensure that mechanisms are in place for the adequate monitoring, oversight, and control of such assistance inside Syria," and requires the Secretary of State to "promptly inform the appropriate congressional committees of each significant instance in which assistance provided pursuant to the authority of this subsection has been compromised, to include the type and amount of assistance affected, a description of the incident and parties involved, and an explanation of the Department of State's response." The latter provision may be of particular interest in light of the reported seizure of U.S. provided assistance by armed groups in December 2013.

> The act further requires the Obama Administration to submit a comprehensive interagency strategy prior to using the authority that would include a "mission statement, achievable objectives and timelines, and a description of inter-agency and donor coordination and implementation of such strategy." The strategy, which may be classified, must also include "a description of oversight and vetting procedures to prevent the misuse of funds." All funds obligated pursuant to the new authority are subject to established congressional notification procedures.
>
> In the 113th Congress, other proposals to authorize the expanded provision of nonlethal and lethal assistance in Syria with various provisos have been considered, including S. 960, the Syria Transition Support Act of 2013, and H.R. 1327, the Free Syria Act of 2013. S. 960 was approved by the Senate Foreign Relations Committee as amended by a 15-3 vote in May 2013.

Efforts to provide lethal assistance to armed opposition elements have similarly evolved and were reported to be expanding in late 2013 amid criticism by some opposition leaders that desired support has not been forthcoming. In June 2013, Deputy National Security Adviser for Strategic Communications Ben Rhodes said that the President had "authorized the expansion of our assistance to the Supreme Military Council," and Secretary of Defense Chuck Hagel said in a September 2013 hearing before the Senate Foreign Relations Committee that the Administration was taking steps to provide arms to some Syrian rebels under covert action authorities.[64] Press reports have cited unidentified U.S. officials suggesting that as of early October 2013, very little lethal equipment had been delivered and fewer than 1,000 opposition fighters had received U.S. supervised training in Jordan. CRS cannot confirm these reports. Press reports further suggested that the program was being enlarged to produce "a few hundred trained fighters each month,"[65] but it is unclear what effect, if any, recent developments, including infighting among opposition groups, have had on any such plans or programs.

To date, U.S. officials have not publicly described in detail which elements of the opposition may be receiving training, what such training may entail, what types of weaponry may be provided in the program, and what safeguards may be in place to monitor the disposition of equipment and the actions of any U.S. trained personnel. In late September, the Administration notified Congress of its intent to use emergency authorities available to the President under the Foreign Assistance Act to provide additional "nonlethal commodities and services" to the SMC. In January, the State Department referred to completed deliveries of food, medical equipment, and vehicles and "planned deliveries of satellite access equipment, laptops, radio communication equipment, and medical kits to moderate SMC elements" in a summary of its nonlethal support efforts to date.[66]

On October 22, Secretary Kerry said that the "London 11" group had "agreed to direct military aid exclusively through the Supreme Military Council ... to curtail the influence of extremists, to isolate the extremists, and to change the balance on the ground."[67] However, as noted above, several prominent Islamist militia groups now coordinate their operations independent of the SMC and have rejected the political and military leadership of the SOC/SMC. Disputes within the SMC over its leadership also may complicate international efforts to engage with the SMC leadership as a conduit for support to moderate armed elements. It remains to be seen whether these realignments, disputes, and policy statements have decisively changed the context in which the United States and its allies are providing support to the armed opposition, or whether or how such support may change in the near future. On April 8, Secretary Kerry told the Senate Foreign Relations Committee that "the fact is we are doing more than we've ever been doing."

OUTLOOK

Looking ahead, U.S. policy makers face a series of difficult choices as they seek to balance their demands that Asad ultimately leave power on the one hand, and their desire for the Syrian government to remain cooperative with implementation of the OPCW Executive Council decision, participate in negotiations with the opposition, and facilitate humanitarian access on the other. By seeking a negotiated rather than a military solution, U.S. policy apparently seeks to bring the conflict to a close while maintaining the security benefits associated with the preservation of some Syrian state institutions. However, recent statements by U.S. officials and other members of the Core Group envision negotiations that will end with the leaders of the current regime having no part in transitional governance in Syria.

As of April 2014, Secretary of State Kerry has acknowledged that President Asad feels more confident in his position and has alluded to a need to change the calculus of the Asad government and the opposition in order to bolster chances for successful negotiations. In testimony before the Senate Foreign Relations Committee on April 8, Secretary Kerry said:

Today, Assad feels fairly secure in Damascus and in some of the corridor going north to the ports. And that's been his strategy. But around him in the south, particularly, in the east and in the north, there is not that kind of security. In fact, the opposition has made some gains recently. And so the key here is - how do you get the parties to a place where they both understand that there isn't going to be a military solution that doesn't destroy the country absolutely and totally, but which ultimately could be negotiated? There has to be a recognition by both of the ripeness of that moment. It's not now. We all understand that. So the question is: Can you do something in order to create that? And that's a legitimate question for the Congress; a legitimate question for the Administration.

Absent a change in conditions that compels Asad's departure or empowers opposition groups to fully depose Asad, current U.S. demands for a negotiated settlement leading to the establishment of a transitional governing body would appear to require the leaders of the current government to agree to leave power voluntarily, which they may continue to resist doing without guarantees of their safety and/or immunity. Opposition members may be unable or unwilling to make such guarantees. U.S. officials have raised the prospect of international peacekeeping arrangements to guarantee elements of a negotiated settlement, but such arrangements could require an international mandate, military forces, and financial contributions that may prove difficult to procure. Meanwhile, powerful armed Islamist opposition forces reject negotiation, seek the creation of an Islamic state, and have vowed to continue fighting until the entire Syrian government is toppled.

Reconciling the current U.S. diplomatic strategy and desire for cooperation on chemical weapons destruction with the simultaneous provision of U.S. assistance to select elements of the opposition may become more difficult in the event that negotiations begin and show promise, or in the event that anti-U.S. Islamist forces or Al Qaeda affiliates make further gains at the expense of their counterparts.

In light of these conditions, responding to the humanitarian needs generated by the crisis and working to prevent the destabilization of Syria's neighbors will remain key agenda items for U.S. decision makers for the foreseeable future.

Armed Conflict in Syria: Overview and U.S. Response

APPENDIX. SELECT GROUP PROFILES

The following descriptions of armed groups operating in Syria are provided as reference estimates compiled, reconciled, and edited by CRS from third-party open-source analysis.[68] CRS cannot independently verify the size, equipment, and current areas of operation of the groups described. In considering these and other analyses of the size, composition, and goals of specific groups there are several factors to consider:

- At present, open source analysis of armed groups operating in Syria relies largely on the self-reporting of individual groups and coalitions. Information is not evenly and regularly available for all groups. Verification is imperfect and is based on independent analysis of self-reported and third party-reported information. Social media outlets and news reports can help verify information, but most analysts consider it to be very difficult to confirm data points.
- There are hundreds of active militia forces, ranging in size from a few dozen to thousands and organized around a wide variety of local communities, ethnic and religious identities, and political-religious ideologies. The size and relative strength of groups have varied and will continue to vary by location and time.
- Trends in the conflict have reflected both diversification and profusion of armed groups and improvement in the size and capabilities of some actors relative to others. Many groups and units who claim to coordinate under various fronts and coalitions in fact appear to operate independently and reserve the right to change allegiances.
- The use of religious or secular imagery and messages by groups may not be reliable indicators of the long term political aims of their members or their likely success in implementing those aims. Factors motivating individuals to support certain groups may not be ideological but practical. For example, the funding available to Islamist groups from various public and private sources in the Persian Gulf may be leading some secular groups to adopt Islamist rhetoric. Others may mask extremist agendas.

Select Anti-Asad Armed Groups

Supreme Military Command Council (SMC) *Leader: Brigadier General Abdul-Ilah al Bashir*
Formation of Supreme Military Command Council (SMC) in December 2012 sought to reorganize non-extremist armed opposition and created regional commands and cooperative committees under the leadership of General Salim Idriss. In February 2014, the SMC voted to replace Idriss as SMC commander with Brigadier General Abdul-Ilah al Bashir, a move that Idriss and some other military commanders have rejected. Members include brigades made up of various combinations of dissident military personnel and civilian recruits, including many forces otherwise identified as members of the "Free Syrian Army" and Islamist militias participating in other coalitions. The direct command authority of the Council leadership and the affiliated Joint Command has not been demonstrated to date. Several regional command members continue to operate their own militia groups independently and in some cases have denounced the political leadership of the Syrian Opposition Coalition (SOC).

Al Jabhat al Islamiya (Islamic Front)
Formed in November 2013, the Islamic Front brings together several of the most powerful Sunni Islamist militia groups in Syria under a shared program, although the full extent and unity of the group and its military command structure remain to be seen. According to the Front's charter, it seeks "the full overthrow of the al Asad regime in Syria and for building an Islamic state ruled by the sharia of God Almighty alone." The Front has attempted to position itself as a relatively moderate coordinating body for likeminded Sunni Islamist opposition groups and as an alternative to the exclusionary and brutal approach of the Al Qaeda-affiliated Islamic State of Iraq and the Levant (ISIL). The Front's charter states that its members believe that force of arms alone will achieve its goal of completely toppling the Asad government, and the Front explicitly rejects the concepts of secularism and a civil state. Its charter states that it will not accept "foreign dictates that undermine its decision-making capabilities" and that it "will not participate in any political activity that violates religion or bestows the power of governance upon anything but the sharia of God Almighty." The following armed groups constitute the core of the Islamic Front and were the original signatories of its charter: Harakat Ahrar al Sham al Islamiya; Saqour al Sham; Ansar al Sham; Jaysh al Islam; Liwa al Tawhid; and Liwa al Haqq.

Harakat Ahrar al Sham al Islamiya (Ahrar al Sham) *Leader: Hassan Abboud*
The "Islamic Movement of the Free Men of the Levant" is a coalition of Salafist-jihadist militias active across Syria. Its statements suggest that its members are motivated by anti-Shiite sectarian views and by support for the establishment of an Islamic state. Ahrar al Sham led the creation of the Syrian Islamic Front (SIF) in December 2012 and then merged with other SIF members, bringing its forces into closer coordination with other similarly minded militias in northern and eastern Syria. In September 2013, terrorism analyst Charles Lister of IHS Janes called the group "arguably the most strategically powerful militant actor in Syria" and credited its humanitarian relief division with being "the most influential militant-run provider of services in Syria." The group subsequently aligned itself with the Islamic Front, and Ahrar al Sham leader Hassan Abboud serves as the head of the Front's political office.

Saqour al Sham *Leader: Ahmed Issa al Sheikh*
Based in northwestern Idlib province, the "Falcons of Syria" are a Salafist-jihadist militia group that calls for the establishment of an Islamic state and has made contradictory statements about Syrian religious minorities. The group's estimated nine thousand fighters are considered by many analysts to be among the more religiously conservative forces within the Islamist faction of the Syrian opposition. Ahmed Issa al Sheikh serves as the overall leader of the Islamic Front.

Jaysh al Islam *Leader: Zahran Alloush*
Based in the Damascus suburbs, the "Army of Islam" (formerly Liwa al Islam or "the Islam Brigade"), is a coalition of Islamist militia led by Salafist figure Zahran Alloush. Alloush's brigade was credited with the July 2012 bomb attack that killed then-Minister of Defense General Dawoud Rajiha and Deputy Defense Minister Assef Shawkat and injured several other prominent regime security officials. After reorganizing the brigade and recruiting others to join an expanded coalition, Alloush launched the Army of Islam and aligned the group with the Islamic Front, of which he serves as the nominal military commander. Prior to the merger, Alloush was reported to receive support from Saudi Arabia and command as many as 5,000 fighters with an arsenal that included armored vehicles.

Figure A-1. Select Anti-Asad Armed Groups.

U.S.-Designated Sunni Terrorist Groups
Jabhat Al Nusra (The Support Front for the People of Syria) *Leader: Abu Mohammad al Golani* A Salafi-jihadist militia, the "Support Front for the People of Syria" emerged in early 2012 and claimed responsibility for a series of high profile suicide bombing attacks against government security forces as well as summary executions of captured regime soldiers. Its leader Abu Mohammed al Golani has stated his allegiance to Al Qaeda leader Ayman al Zawahiri, and the group's messaging, tactics, and ideology mirror those of Al Qaeda affiliates in other regional conflict zones. Unofficial estimates suggest it may have as many as 6,000 fighters operating across Syria. Reporting from Syria suggests that Al Nusra Front members have been coordinating with other opposition factions in northern and southern Syria, but not always consistently or successfully. Nusra members engage in organized relief work and service provision efforts to curry favor with civilians, and the group positioned itself as a mediator during January 2014 clashes between other opposition groups and the more uncompromisingly violent Islamic State of Iraq and the Levant. The prospect for clashes between Al Nusra and other groups remains, as the Front's uncompromising views on the long-term implementation of Islamic religious law may create rifts with other Sunni Arabs and Kurds, not to mention religious minorities. The United States has designated Al Nusra as a Foreign Terrorist Organization (FTO) and two of its leaders as Specially Designated Global Terrorists acting on behalf of Al Qaeda in Iraq (also an FTO) pursuant to Executive Order 13224.
The Islamic State in Iraq and the Levant (ISIL) *Leader: Abu Bakr al Baghdadi* Estimates of ISIL strength in Syria vary, but some observers believe ISIL may have had as many as 4,000 fighters in the field prior to the January 2014 outbreak of hostilities with other opposition forces. Its main areas of operation are in northern and eastern Syria near the borders of Turkey and Iraq, although ISIL fighters also are reported to operate in and around Homs and on the outskirts of Damascus, with less of a reported presence in southern Syria. ISIL fighters have engaged in sectarian attacks against Shiite and Christian religious sites and individuals suspected of being Shiite fighters. After taking control of the town of Raqqa, ISIL moved to control a key border crossing with Turkey at Azaz, north of Aleppo, and impose themselves in other areas of Idlib and Aleppo provinces. ISIL clashed with Kurdish and other Arab militia groups in the north prior to January 2014, and the outbreak of widespread hostilities with other opposition forces has appeared to result in the ISIL sustaining considerable tactical losses. ISIL's strategic prospects appear less certain than they did prior to the fighting, but the group had not been defeated. ISIL has been reported to include hundreds of foreign fighters affiliated with the Jaysh al Muhajirin wal Ansar (the Army of Expatriates and Supporters), although foreign fighters were reported to be especially targeted by groups angered by ISIL's extremism and violent tactics.

Figure A-2. U.S.-Designated Sunni Terrorist Groups.

End Notes

[1] See for example, Charles Lister, "Syria's insurgency beyond Good Guys and Bad Guys," ForeignPolicy.com, Middle East Channel (blog), September 20, 2013, and, Aron Lund, "The Politics of the Islamic Front 1: Structure and Support," Carnegie Endowment for International Peace, Syria in Crisis (blog), January 14, 2014.

[2] President Asad, interview with Agence France Press, Syrian Arab News Agency, January 21, 2014.

[3] Asad, speech at the Damascus Opera House, Syrian Arab News Agency, January 6, 2013.

[4] Secretary of State John Kerry, Press Statement: Geneva Conference and Situation in Syria, Washington, DC, February 16, 2014.

[5] Syrian Arab News Agency (SANA), "Al-Jaafari: we will spare no efforts to make Geneva rounds of talks a success with open-mindedness and a positive spirit," Damascus, Syria, February 16, 2014.

[6] Transcript of Press Conference by Joint Special Representative for Syria (JSRS) Lakhdar Brahimi, Geneva, Switzerland, February 15, 2014.

[7] Secretary of State John Kerry, Intervention at the Geneva II International Conference on Syria, January 22, 2014.

[8] The Islamic State of Iraq and the Levant (ISIL) also is commonly referred to in English language reports as the Islamic State of Iraq and Al Sham (ISIS). *Al Sham* is an Arabic term for the Levant. Some Syrians refer to ISIL as "Daesh," its Arabic acronym.

[9] Remarks by James R. Clapper, Director of National Intelligence, to the Senate Armed Services Committee, February 11, 2014.

[10] Office of the Director for National Intelligence, *Worldwide Threat Assessment of the U.S. Intelligence Community*, Senate Select Committee on Intelligence, January 29, 2014.

[11] Office of the Director for National Intelligence, *Worldwide Threat Assessment of the U.S. Intelligence Community*, Senate Select Committee on Intelligence, January 29, 2014.

[12] For details on U.S. humanitarian assistance see USAID, Syria Complex Emergency Fact Sheet #11, Fiscal Year (FY) 2014, March 27, 2014. Some U.S. aid to opposition forces and some humanitarian assistance were placed on hold in December 2013, as fighting in northern Syria disrupted mechanisms put in place to monitor and secure U.S. supplies.

[13] For more information, see UNOCHA Syria Humanitarian Assistance Response Plan (SHARP) 2014 and 2014 Regional Response Plan (RRP).

[14] The following armed groups constitute the core of the Islamic Front and were the original signatories of its charter: Ahrar al Sham Islamic Movement; Suqur al Sham Brigades; Ansar al Sham Battalions; Jaysh al Islam; Liwa al Tawhid; and Liwa al Haqq.

[15] Charter of the Islamic Front. For translation, see U.S. Government Open Source Center (OSC) Document TRR2013112671951889, Syria: New 'Islamic Front' Formation Releases Charter, November 26, 2013.

[16] The signatories—The Islamic Front, the Mujahedin Army, and the Islamic Union for the Soldiers of the Levant— refer to themselves as the "forces active on the ground" in contrast to "those who only represent themselves." OSC Document TRR2014012066474330, "Syria: IF, Others Reject Regime Presence at Geneva 2, Issue Conditions for Political Solution," January 20, 2014.

[17] The group consists of: Egypt, France, Germany, Italy, Jordan, Qatar, Saudi Arabia, Turkey, the United Arab Emirates, the United Kingdom, and the United States.

[18] Foreign Ministry of France, Declaration of the Core Group Ministerial Meeting on Syria, Paris, January 12, 2014.

[19] Testimony of CIA Director John Brennan, House Permanent Select Committee on Intelligence, February 5, 2014.

[20] Ben Hubbard, "Syria Proposes Aleppo Cease-Fire…" *New York Times*, January 17, 2014.

[21] OSC Report GMP20120721586002, "Islamic State of Iraq Amir Calls on Sunni Tribes To 'Repent,'" July 21, 2012.

[22] OSC Report TRR2014011980831299, "Statement by ISIL Emir Condemning 'War' Against Group," Jan. 19, 2014.

[23] Prepared by Carla Humud, Analyst in Middle Eastern and African Affairs.

[24] "Syrian army to impose blockade in Aleppo," *Al Monitor*, March 5, 2014; and "Syrian army, Hezbollah storm Yabrud," *Daily Star*, March 15, 2014.

[25] "Syria plans presidential elections in summer; minister says Assad will likely be one of several candidates," *Wall Street Journal*, March 16, 2014.

[26] "Syrians have decided that Asad should run in elections: minister," Reuters, January 7, 2014; and, Office of the Director for National Intelligence, *Worldwide Threat Assessment of the U.S. Intelligence Community*, Senate Select Committee on Intelligence, January 29, 2014.

[27] Syrian Arab News Agency, "President al-Assad gives interview to the German *Frankfurter Allgemeine Zeitung* newspaper," June 17, 2013.

[28] "Syrian presidential election law excludes most opposition leaders," *Reuters*, March 14, 2014.

[29] Joint Statement by the London 11 Countries, April 3, 2014.

[30] "Iran and Hezbollah build militia networks in Syria in event that Asad falls," *Washington Post*, February 10, 2013.

[31] E.O. 13582, U.S. Department of Treasury, August 10, 2012.

Armed Conflict in Syria: Overview and U.S. Response

[32] "Hezbollah leader Nasrallah vows to keep fighters in Syria," *BBC*, February 16, 2014; and, OSC Report LIR2014040766062493, "Lebanon's Nasrallah to Al-Safir: Risk of Bombings Drops, Danger of Syrian Regime's Fall Ends," *Al Safir* Online (Beirut), April 7, 2014.

[33] "Drastic rise in Hezbollah death toll as party battles for Yabroud," *The Daily Star*, March 10, 2014.

[34] "Israel watches warily as Hezbollah gains battle skills in Syria," *New York Times*, March 10, 2014.

[35] "Syrian Army goes all-in to take back strategic highway," *Christian Science Monitor*, December 2, 2013.

[36] "Hezbollah and the fight for control in Qalamoun," Institute for the Study of War, November 26, 2013.

[37] "Hezbollah undeterred by ISIS claim, threats," *Daily Star*, January 6, 2014.

[38] "Leaked video: Iran guiding thousands of Shiite fighters to Syria," *Christian Science Monitor*, September 23, 2013; "From Qusair to Yabrud: Shiite foreign fighters in Syria," *Al Monitor*, March 6, 2014.

[39] "From Karbala to Sayyida Zaynab: Iraqi Fighters in Syria's Shi'a Militias," CTC Sentinel, August 27, 2013.

[40] "From Karbala to Sayyida Zaynab: Iraqi Fighters in Syria's Shi'a Militias," CTC Sentinel, August 27, 2013.

[41] "Iraqi Shi'ites flock to Assad's side as sectarian split widens," *Reuters*, June 19, 2013.

[42] Department of the Treasury, Press Release, February 16, 2012.

[43] "Elite Iranian unit's commander says his forces are in Syria," *Washington Post*, September 16, 2012.

[44] "From Qusair to Yabrud: Shiite foreign fighters in Syria," *Al Monitor*, March 6, 2014.

[45] "Iranians dial up presence in Syria," *Wall Street Journal*, September 16, 2013.

[46] Prepared by Mary Beth Nikitin, Specialist in Nonproliferation.

[47] See http://opcw.unmissions.org/.

[48] "Army to Destroy Syrian Chemical Weapons Aboard Ship," *Army News Service*, January 3, 2014.

[49] "NATO to cancel activities with Russia, step up military cooperation with Ukraine," *Stars and Stripes*, March 6, 2014.

[50] "OPCW awards contracts to two companies for destruction of Syrian chemical and effluents," OPCW-U.N. Joint Mission Press Release February 14, 2014, http://opcw.unmissions.org/ AboutOPCWUNJointMission/tabid/54/ctl/ Details/mid/651/ItemID/182/Default.aspx

[51] "Director General says Removal of Priority Chemicals in Syria Marks Important New Phase in Work of Joint Mission," OPCW press release, January 8, 2014.

[52] Nick Cumming-Bruce and Rick Gladstone, "Syrian Government Reports 2 Attacks on Chemical Arms Sites," *New York Times*, January 8, 2014.

[53] Robert P. Mikulak, "Statement to the Thirty-Ninth Meeting of the Executive Council," The Hague, Netherlands, February 21, 2014.

[54] "Over half of Syria's chemical weapons removed or destroyed, says joint OPCW-UN mission," UN News Centre, March 20, 2014.

[55] Ibid.; Secretary of State John Kerry Testimony before the Senate Foreign Relations Committee, April 8, 2014.

[56] "Syria to miss deadline to destroy 12 chemical arms sites," *Reuters*, March 6, 2014.

[57] http://www.state.gov/t/avc/rls/2014/221891.htm.

[58] http://opcw.unmissions.org/Portals/opcw-un-syria/General%20FAQs%20for%20PDF.pdf.

[59] Other competing foreign policy priorities also have influenced the Administration's position, such as a desire to maintain Russian and Chinese support for international sanctions on Iran's nuclear program and concern that sectarian and strategic competition in Syria could ignite a regional conflict and threaten U.S. allies and global security interests.

[60] See U.S. State Department Fact Sheet, U.S. Assistance and Support for the Transition, January 17, 2014; and Assistant Secretary of State for Near East Affairs Anne Patterson Testimony before the Senate Foreign Relations Committee, March 26, 2014.

[61] The State Department has reported that lines of supply for nonlethal support to armed opposition elements are "periodically contested by the regime or extremist fighters." In the wake of the incident the Obama Administration "decided that it was a risk to be providing that assistance if it's going to the extremists." However, on January 12, Secretary Kerry said the Administration is "considering the renewal of that assistance to the opposition," and referred to "augmented support to the opposition" in remarks in Montreux, Switzerland, on January 22. See Secretary of State Kerry, Remarks with Qatari Foreign Minister Khalid bin Muhammad al Atiyah, Paris, France, January 12, 2014; and, Secretary of State Kerry, Press Availability at the Geneva II International Conference on Syria, January 22, 2014.

[62] Statement of U.S. State Department Spokesperson Marie Harf, Press Briefing, Washington, DC, December 16, 2013.

[63] OSC Document TRR2013112671951889.

[64] Secretary Hagel said, "it was June of this year that the president made the decision to support lethal assistance to the opposition. As you all know, we have been very supportive with hundreds of millions of dollars of non-lethal assistance. The vetting process that Secretary Kerry noted has been significant, but—I'll ask General Dempsey if he wants to add anything—but we, the Department of Defense, have not been directly involved in this. This is, as you know, a covert action. And, as Secretary Kerry noted, probably to [go] into much more detail would—would require a closed or classified hearing."

[65] Greg Miller, "CIA ramping up covert training program for moderate Syrian rebels," Washington Post, October 2, 2013; and, Adam Entous and Nour Malas, "U.S. Still Hasn't Armed Syrian Rebels," Wall Street Journal, September 4, 2013.

[66] Office of the State Department Spokesperson, "The Syrian Crisis: U.S. Assistance and Support for the Transition," January 17, 2014

[67] Remarks of Secretary of State John Kerry, London, United Kingdom, October 22, 2013.

[68] CRS consulted the following sources and others while preparing the analysis below: Facebook, Twitter, and YouTube outlets associated with groups. Charles Lister, "Syria's insurgency beyond Good Guys and Bad Guys," ForeignPolicy.com, Middle East Channel (blog), September 20, 2013. Charles Lister, "Syria's Insurgent Landscape," IHS Jane's Terrorism and Security Monitor/IHS Jane's Terrorism & Insurgency Centre, September 2013. Aron Lund, "The Non-State Militant Landscape in Syria," U.S. Military Academy Combatting Terrorism Center, CTC Sentinel, August 2013. Ian Black, "Saudi Arabia to spend millions to train new rebel force," The Guardian (UK), November 7, 2013. Michael Weiss, "Mergers and Acquisitions," NOW. Online (Lebanon), October 29, 2013. OSC Document PLN2013100218082086, "Syria: Chief of Newly Formed 'Jaysh al-Islam' Coalition Interviewed on Al-Qa'ida Ties, Geneva II," Al Jazirah Live Satellite Television (Doha) in Arabic, September 20, 2013. Aron Lund, "Islamist Groups Declare Opposition to National Coalition and U.S. Strategy," Syria Comment (blog), September 24-5, 2013. OSC Document TRR2013112671951889, "Syria: New 'Islamic Front' Formation Releases Charter," November 26, 2013. Aron Lund, "Say Hello to the Islamic Front," Carnegie Endowment for International Peace, Syria in Crisis (blog), November 22, 2013. Aaron Y. Zelin, "Rebels Consolidating Strength in Syria: The Islamic Front," Washington Institute for Near East Policy, PolicyWatch 2177, December 3, 2013.

In: Internal Conflict Regions in the Middle East ISBN: 978-1-63321-259-6
Editor: Dana V. Gray © 2014 Nova Science Publishers, Inc.

Chapter 3

SYRIA: OVERVIEW OF THE HUMANITARIAN RESPONSE[*]

Rhoda Margesson and Susan G. Chesser

SUMMARY

The ongoing conflict that began in March 2011 in Syria has created one of the most pressing humanitarian crises in the world. Three years later, as of early March 2014, an estimated 9.3 million people inside Syria, nearly half the population, have been affected by the conflict. It is estimated that there are 6.5 million displaced persons inside Syria and 2.5 million Syrians displaced as refugees, with 97% fleeing to countries in the immediate surrounding region, including Turkey, Lebanon, Jordan, Iraq, Egypt, and other parts of North Africa. The situation is fluid and continues to worsen, while humanitarian needs are immense and increase daily.

While internationally supervised disarmament of chemical weapons in Syria is proceeding, albeit with some difficulty, U.S. and international diplomatic efforts to negotiate a political end to the fighting in Syria opened on January 22, 2014, in Montreux, Switzerland. The "Geneva II" talks include some members of the Syrian opposition, representatives of the Syrian government, and other government leaders. The first round of talks came to an

---

[*] This is an edited, reformatted and augmented version of a Congressional Research Service publication R43119, prepared for Members and Committees of Congress dated March 13, 2014.

end on January 31 and resumed February 10-15, but ended with little progress in efforts to end the civil war. The parties reportedly agreed to an agenda for a third round of talks. Many experts and observers hoped that a lasting agreement would have been reached on "humanitarian pauses" to allow access and relief to thousands of civilians blockaded in towns and cities in Syria. On February 22, the U.N. Security Council unanimously adopted Resolution 2139 (2014) to increase humanitarian access and aid delivery in Syria.

U.S. Assistance and Priorities

The United States is the largest donor of humanitarian assistance and is part of the massive, international humanitarian operation in parts of Syria and in neighboring countries. Beginning in FY2012, through March 13, 2014, the United States has allocated more than $1.7 billion to meet humanitarian needs using existing funding from global humanitarian accounts and some reprogrammed funding. U.S. humanitarian policy is guided by concerns about humanitarian access and protection within Syria; the large refugee flows out of the country that strain the resources of neighboring countries (and could negatively impact the overall stability of the region); and a protracted and escalating humanitarian emergency. The Administration's FY2015 budget request seeks $1.1 billion in humanitarian assistance for Syria and the region.

International Response

The international humanitarian response is massive and complex and struggles to keep pace with urgent developments that have escalated well beyond anticipated needs and continue to do so. Access within Syria is severely constrained by violence and restrictions imposed by the Syrian government on the operations of humanitarian organizations. In mid-December 2013, the United Nations launched two appeals—taken together its largest appeal in history—requesting $6.5 billion in contributions to meet the ongoing humanitarian needs in Syria and the region.

Ongoing Humanitarian Challenges of the Syria Crisis and U.S. Policy

As U.S. policy makers and the international community deliberate over what, if any, actions they can or should take on the Syria crisis, possible humanitarian policy issues for Congress include

- the immediate need for access within Syria by humanitarian organizations, which has been severely constrained by violence and restrictions imposed by the Syrian government;
- examining U.S. assistance and priorities in an ongoing humanitarian response;
- balancing the Syria response with domestic priorities and other humanitarian concerns worldwide;
- ensuring the ongoing willingness and cooperation of Syria's neighbors, which are receiving the vast majority of refugees from Syria, to keep borders open and to host refugees fleeing Syria;
- finding ways to alleviate the strain on civilians and those responding to the crisis as the situation worsens and becomes more protracted, including the support of initiatives, such as emergency development assistance, for communities within neighboring countries that are hosting refugees; and
- encouraging the participation of other countries to provide support through humanitarian admission, resettlement, facilitated visa procedures, and protection for those seeking asylum.

The United States has a critical voice regarding humanitarian access in Syria, the pace of humanitarian developments and contingency planning, support to neighboring countries that are hosting refugees, and burdensharing among donors.

OVERVIEW AND RECENT DEVELOPMENTS[1]

Congress has demonstrated an ongoing interest in many different aspects of the three-year civil war in Syria. The humanitarian situation, in particular, has garnered significant bipartisan attention. Members have proposed and enacted legislation addressing the issue and have held hearings on the U.S. and international humanitarian response to the conflict. Although not discussed in this report, the use of chemical weapons in Syria on August 21, 2013, triggered an intense debate over possible U.S. military intervention.[2] This debate created temporary momentum focused on the dire humanitarian situation within Syrian where humanitarian organizations remain severely constrained by the conflict, fighting, and restrictions imposed by the Syrian government.

Humanitarian assistance has traditionally been one of the least controversial types of foreign aid, and in the Syria context, it has so far been one avenue in which the United States has provided support to Syrian civilians absent a political solution. The United States remains the largest humanitarian donor. As of early March 2014, it is providing roughly 42% of the funding for the humanitarian response in calendar year (CY) 2014, but with an average of 25% in CY2012-CY2013. U.S. humanitarian policy is guided by concerns about access and protection within Syria; the large refugee flows out of the country that strain the resources of neighboring countries (and could negatively impact the overall stability of the region); and an already escalating and protracted humanitarian emergency.

ESTIMATED NUMBERS AT A GLANCE (AS OF FEBRUARY 26, 2014)

Syria's total population:
21.4 million
Number in need of humanitarian assistance:
9.3 million (of these, **over 3 million** are in hard-to-reach and besieged areas)
Number of children affected by the crisis in Syria:
5.5 million
Number of Internally Displaced Persons (IDPs) within Syria:
6.5 million
Number of refugees fleeing Syria and seeking protection in neighboring countries and North Africa:
2.5 million

Source: Humanitarian Bulletin, Syrian Arab Republic, Issue 43, February 26, 2014, United Nations Office for the Coordination of Humanitarian Affairs.

Syria: Overview of the Humanitarian Response

Along with the international community, the United States provides humanitarian assistance to civilians affected by the conflict both inside and outside Syria. Such assistance includes medical care and medical supplies (including immunization programs), food, water, shelter, and other non-food items such as blankets and clothing. It also supports programs focused on psycho-social rehabilitation of refugees and the prevention of gender-based violence.[3]

Since the conflict began in March 2011 in Syria, reportedly an unknown number of civilians have been wounded and tens of thousands of lives lost. Some observers estimate the death toll figures to be as many as 100,000 to 130,000, and others say it is likely much higher.[4] In January 2014, according to press reports, the United Nations planned to stop updating the death toll from the Syria conflict, apparently due to the fact that it could no longer verify the sources of information that led to the last count of 100,000 (July 2013). It is estimated that more than 2% of the pre-conflict Syrian population of 21.4 million has been killed, maimed, or wounded over the course of the conflict.

In addition, allegations by human rights groups of serious human rights violations have emerged over the past two years and increased dramatically in recent months. Observers claim that hundreds of detainees and political prisoners have died under torture. The U.N. Independent International Commission of Inquiry on the Syrian Arab Republic pointed to the "reckless manner in which parties to the conflict conduct hostilities" as a main cause of the civilian casualties and displacement.[5] The International Committee of the Red Cross (ICRC) has repeatedly urged all sides to fully comply with international humanitarian law. The ICRC currently has no access to visit detainees. The United States and many other countries have increasingly recognized the human rights crisis, which not only exacerbates the humanitarian situation, but raises the prospect that atrocities reaching the level of crimes against humanity and war crimes by armed groups may have been committed, including the use of chemical weapons that killed (by some reports) as many as 1,400 civilians on August 21.[6] On January 17, 2014, High Commissioner for Human Rights Navi Pillay condemned the obstruction of food and medical deliveries to those living in the Yarmouk Palestinian refugee camp, emphasizing that starving civilians as a method of combat was prohibited under international law. Other reports of mass executions of detainees on the one hand and killing of civilians on the other have also generated condemnation. Outside Syria, humanitarian workers have observed a sharp rise in gender-based crimes, including rape and sexual violence, as well as exploitation and discrimination in refugee camps and informal settlements.

The Independent International Commission of Inquiry on the Syrian Arab Republic was established on August 22, 2011, by the Human Rights Council.[7] Its mandate is to investigate all alleged violations of international human rights law since March 2011 in the Syrian Arab Republic. The commission was also tasked with (1) establishing the facts and circumstances of such violations and (2) of the crimes perpetrated and, where possible, to identify those responsible with a view of ensuring that perpetrators of violations, including those that may constitute crimes against humanity, are held accountable.[8]

The short- to medium-term outlook for the resolution of the conflict in Syria and impact on its neighbors is not positive. The United States and other third parties face a number of difficult policy choices with limited potential to decisively shape the overall outcome. These issues are addressed in other CRS reports. As the international community deliberates over what action it can or should take on the crisis, a massive humanitarian operation continues in parts of Syria and in neighboring countries.

Selected International Efforts

On October 2, 2013, the U.N. Security Council issued a Presidential Statement urging Syrian authorities "to facilitate the expansion of humanitarian relief operations and lift bureaucratic impediments and other obstacles in Syria."[9] Although non-binding, the wide-ranging statement indicated that the Council members recognized the deterioration of the humanitarian situation and the need to address particular elements, including access. As of the end of January 2014, over 3 million people were estimated to be living in hard-to-reach areas or those besieged by either the Government of Syria or opposition forces.[10] Moreover, reports of intentional policies of starvation in areas under siege by the government, attacks against civilians and indiscriminant use of heavy weapons, and a weak health infrastructure that is often under deliberate attack illustrate the dire conditions under which civilians are trying to survive.

Valerie Amos, U.N. Under Secretary General for Humanitarian Affairs and Emergency Relief Coordinator, U.N. Office for the Coordination of Humanitarian Assistance (UNOCHA), last briefed U.N. Security Council members on December 3, 2013. On December 31, Amos condemned the attacks against civilians in Aleppo and raised concerns about the government's indiscriminant use of heavy weapons. In a January 17, 2014, note to Council members, she acknowledged incremental progress in some situations, but emphasized the intense needs of civilians in besieged areas. For months, Amos has publicly called for all parties to end the violence, allow access for aid organizations, and "respect their obligations under international human rights and humanitarian law."

The "Geneva II" talks in Switzerland, which include some members of the Syrian opposition, representatives of the Syrian government, and other government leaders, were launched on January 22, 2014. The first round came to an end on January 31. Many experts and observers hoped that a lasting agreement would have been reached on "humanitarian pauses" to allow access and relief to thousands of civilians blockaded in towns and cities in Syria. On February 6, 2014, a representative of the U.N. Secretary-General "welcomed the reports that the Syrian parties have agreed to a humanitarian pause to allow civilians out of, and aid into, Old Homs City."[11] The United Nations and its humanitarian partners prepositioned food and medical supplies on the outskirts of the besieged city with staff on standby to assist as a temporary ceasefire allowed some access, delivery of aid, and evacuations of civilians. A second round of the Geneva II talks took place in Switzerland between February 10-15, but ended with little progress in efforts to end the civil war. The parties reportedly agreed to an agenda for a third round of talks.

On February 22, 2014, the U.N. Security Council unanimously adopted Resolution 2139 (2014) to increase humanitarian access and aid delivery in Syria. The resolution demands that "all parties, in particular the Syrian authorities, promptly allow rapid, safe and unhindered humanitarian access for U.N. humanitarian agencies and their implementing partners, including across conflict lines and across borders."[12] The five-page resolution is comprehensive in its statement about the humanitarian situation, specifically addressing the impact on civilians in Syria and the region, and the efforts of host countries, the United Nations, and humanitarian actors to respond to the crisis. It also condemns the violations of human rights and international humanitarian law; demands the end to all forms of violence, the cessation of attacks against civilians, and indiscriminate use of weapons; and calls for the implementation of the aforementioned October 2, 2013 statement by the President of the Security Council.[13]

In addition, it calls on parties to lift the sieges of populated areas and allow the delivery of food and medicine. Citing the Syrian authorities in particular, the Council urges all parties "to take all appropriate steps to facilitate the efforts of the United Nations, specialized agencies, and all humanitarian actors engaged in humanitarian relief activities, to provide immediate humanitarian assistance to the affected people in Syria." The resolution touches on medical neutrality, protection of civilians, detention and torture, and security of aid workers. It demands an end to impunity for violations of international humanitarian law, and condemns the rise of Al-Qaeda-affiliated terrorist attacks. The Council requests that the Secretary-General submit a report to it every 30 days on the implementation of the resolution and expresses "its intent to take further steps in the case of non-compliance."

On February 25, 2014, the U.N. General Assembly held an informal briefing on the humanitarian situation in Syria, at which the Secretary-General delivered remarks. Other senior officials also spoke at the meeting.[14]

EVOLVING HUMANITARIAN SITUATION

The humanitarian situation in Syria and in neighboring countries is dire. As conditions inside Syria continue to deteriorate, UNOCHA estimates that of an overall population of just fewer than 21.4 million, nearly 50% (9.3 million people) are in need of humanitarian assistance, including between 6.5 million displaced inside Syria.[15] The number of Syrians that have been displaced as refugees, primarily to countries in the immediate surrounding region, is estimated to be 2.5 million.

Situation in Syria

Intense fighting and violence, population displacement, lack of basic public services, and economic collapse drive the humanitarian crisis. In recent months, cities and towns in Syria under siege by the government or opposition forces have added a layer of desperation for an estimated 3 million civilians trapped and without access to humanitarian assistance. The conflict has brought out social, political, and sectarian tensions among Syrians in general amid concerns for minority groups in particular. The destruction of housing and infrastructure (hospitals, schools) combined with economic collapse has affected most Syrians. Food, water, sanitation, medical assistance, shelter, and essential non-food items are critically needed, particularly in areas that have seen intense fighting. Winter conditions have only compounded the situation. In addition, other critical health concerns, such as the outbreak of polio have highlighted the consequences of war and challenges faced by a vulnerable population.

The number of Internally Displaced Persons (IDPs)—estimated to be 6.5 million—is very fluid. Many Syrians, some of whom have been displaced multiple times, leave their homes to escape violence and then return when conflict in their area decreases. It is not clear how many IDPs are affected by repeat displacements, nor if, or how often, they are included in IDP counts. Many IDPs stay in unofficial shelters, unfinished buildings, makeshift accommodations, and unofficial camps. IDPs are predominantly women, children, and the elderly.

Syria also hosts refugees from elsewhere, and these populations have been vulnerable to the conflict. Of the estimated 530,000 Palestinian refugees living in Syria, approximately 420,000 require humanitarian assistance, of which 235,000—nearly half of the original number of Palestinian refugees hosted by Syria—have been internally displaced. In addition, Palestinian refugees have approached the U.N. Relief and Works Agency for Palestine Refugees in the Near East (UNRWA) in Lebanon and a much smaller number have registered with UNRWA in Jordan. There have been reports of some Palestinian refugees finding their way to Gaza, Egypt, and Turkey, and in smaller numbers to Malaysia, Thailand, and Indonesia.

Reportedly, Palestinian refugees in Syria are disproportionally and increasingly vulnerable. Many are living in areas that have seen intense fighting; they have nowhere to go within Syria and external flight options are limited. A case in point is the Yarmouk refugee camp near Damascus. From a pre-conflict population of about 160,000, there are approximately 18,000 Palestinians (and possibly non-Palestinian civilians) in the camp. Yarmouk has been under siege and little to no humanitarian access has been possible for months, despite UNRWA's calls for continuous, uninterrupted access. On January 30, 2014, a U.N. convoy entered Yarmouk and distributed food parcels, the first major distribution since July 2013.

Syria also hosts approximately 68,000 registered refugees who originate mainly from Iraq, Afghanistan, Somalia, and Sudan. Other vulnerable populations include third country nationals and vulnerable migrants. At this point it is not known how many of the refugee and vulnerable populations have been displaced. Moreover, these numbers do not account for populations who may have been living in Syria, but were not registered as refugees. For example, it is thought that 1 million or more Iraqis fled to Syria from Iraq between 2003 and 2006; current estimates suggest this number is now approximately 500,000, of which about 10% are registered with UNHCR.

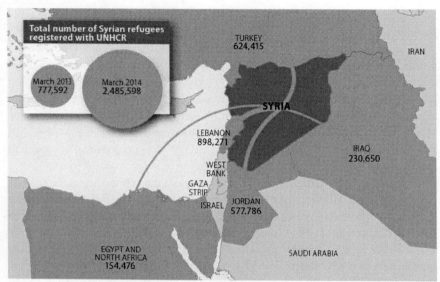

Source: Created by CRS, with numbers from the Syria Regional Refugee Response, U.N. High Commissioner for Refugees, http://data.unhcr.org/syrianrefugees/regional.php, as viewed on March 3, 2014.

Figure 1. Dispersal of Refugees from Syria.

Situation in Neighboring Countries

The threat of a fragmented Syria and difficult challenges for neighboring countries hosting refugees have created a fragile security and political environment. As of early March 2014, an estimated 2.5 million Syrians have been forced to flee the violence and conflict with 97% seeking refuge in countries in the immediate surrounding region, primarily Lebanon, Jordan, Turkey, Iraq, Egypt, and in other parts of North Africa. The number of registered refugees (or those awaiting registration) has increased dramatically.[16] Many observers are predicting a further spike in the number of displaced persons. Experts recognize that this number is likely much higher as some Syrians have not registered, presumably from fear or other reasons, and have chosen instead to blend in with the local population, living in rented accommodations and makeshift shelters, particularly in towns and cities.

The added economic, energy, and natural resource pressures of large Syrian refugee populations weigh heavily on neighboring countries, particularly in Lebanon, Jordan, and Turkey. Palestinian refugees from Syria also complicate the underlying political dynamics of Lebanon and Jordan, where large Palestinian refugee populations already reside. The governments of countries hosting refugees have concerns about the potential political implications of allowing displaced populations to remain, especially for a protracted period of time.

The types of assistance and shelter options available to refugees vary in the countries that are hosting them. In Turkey, Jordan, and Iraq, there are 24 refugee camps and new camps are under construction. In camps, assistance is provided by host governments and the international community, and there are concerns about overcrowding and the risk of disease. However, the U.N. Office for the Coordination of Humanitarian Assistance (UNOCHA) estimates that the majority of Syrian refugees (more than 80%) are living outside camps in mostly urban settings. The impact on many host communities has become overwhelming. Overcrowded schools, inadequate hospital services, impacts on resources such as water—all contribute to the burden for neighboring countries. Urgent priorities include protecting vulnerable refugees from violence and meeting their basic needs.

One of the biggest challenges is shelter. The refugees outside of camps face high rental rates, overcrowding, and competition for space in addition to other living expenses and limited, if any, work opportunities. The onset of winter only compounded the challenges these populations face. Urban refugees are often invisible and difficult to identify and assist.

Jordan, Lebanon, and Turkey host the vast majority of the displaced populations outside Syria. (See **Figure 2**.) The United States and the international community have recognized the contribution of those countries hosting refugees and supported their efforts, while encouraging them to keep their borders open to those fleeing conflict in Syria. At different times during the conflict, the number of refugees crossing into neighboring countries has decreased at some border points because refugee-hosting countries have taken steps to restrict the flow, causing those fleeing Syria to be stranded inside its border areas.

U.S. POLICY

The Obama Administration has consistently supported providing humanitarian assistance to all civilians affected by the conflict in Syria. It is working closely with neighboring countries, other governments, the United

Nations, and humanitarian partners in its response to the crisis. Congress has also demonstrated sustained interest and bipartisan support for a robust U.S. humanitarian response, although Members may be divided over other dimensions of U.S. policy.[17]

U.S. humanitarian priorities in Syria include

- providing as much humanitarian assistance as possible through partners and multilateral mechanisms;
- supporting protection activities for vulnerable populations;
- helping to develop a strong multilateral response to support countries hosting refugees;
- encouraging donor pledges and contributions; and
- building capacity within Syria and among its neighbors for immediate assistance and contingency planning for what has become a protracted crisis.

(An additional 48,378 persons are awaiting registration as of March 3, 2014.)

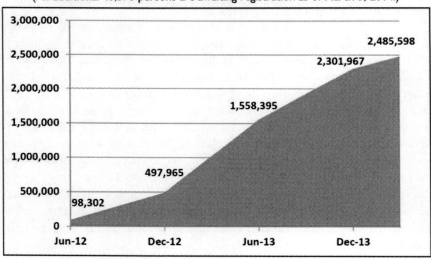

Source: Compiled by CRS from information provided by the United Nations High Commissioner for Refugees at its Inter-agency Information sharing Portal on the Syria Regional Refugee Response at http://data.unhcr.org/syrianrefugees/regional.php.

Note: All figures are taken from the 30th day of the month, every six months, except the last number, which was taken on March 1, 2014.

Figure 2. Number of Syrian Refugees Registered with the United Nations High Commissioner for Refugees (UNHCR) in Egypt, Iraq, Jordan, Lebanon, Turkey, and Northern Africa.

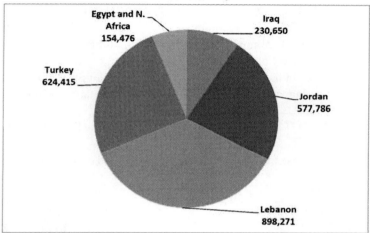

Source: Syria Regional Refugee Response, United Nations High Commissioner for Refugees, http://data.unhcr.org/syrianrefugees/regional.php.
Note: North Africa countries include Morocco, Algeria, and Libya.

Figure 3. Distribution of Refugees, by Country.

The Bureau for Democracy, Conflict, and Humanitarian Assistance (DCHA) of the U.S. Agency for International Development (USAID) and the State Department's Bureau of Population, Refugees, and Migration (PRM) coordinate U.S. humanitarian assistance for Syria.

U.S. Funding and Allocation

Beginning in FY2012, through March 13, 2014, the United States has allocated more than $1.7 billion for humanitarian activities both inside Syria and in neighboring countries, which includes the most recent announcement of $380 million in additional U.S. humanitarian assistance to help those affected by the crisis.[18] The U.S. contribution has been allocated in response to U.N. humanitarian appeals, as well as supporting other projects using existing funding from global humanitarian accounts and some reprogrammed funding.[19]

See **Appendix A** for a selected list of implementing partners receiving U.S. funding in FY2014.

U.S. assistance is distributed based on need throughout all 14 governorates of Syria. The United States is working through a number of channels to provide this assistance, including U.N. entities, non-governmental organizations (NGOs), community-based partners, and the Syrian Opposition Coalition's Assistance Coordination Unit. In addition, the United States works with host countries in the region that support the influx of Syrian refugees. The distribution of its humanitarian assistance is listed in the tables below.

Table 1. Total U.S. Humanitarian Assistance to the Syria Complex Emergency, FY2012–FY2014
(For Needs in Syria and Neighboring Countries [as of March 13, 2014])

U.S. Agency	Amount
USAID/Office of Foreign Disaster Assistance (OFDA)	$370,986,181
USAID/Food For Peace (FFP)	$530,699,121
State Department/Bureau of Population, Refugees and Migration (PRM)	$838,084,221
Total	**$1,739,769,523**

Source: USAID, "Syria–Complex Emergency" Fact Sheet #10, Fiscal Year (FY) 2014, March 13, 2014.

Note: Global humanitarian accounts include International Disaster Assistance (IDA), Migration and Refugee Assistance (MRA), Emergency Refugee and Migration Assistance (ERMA) and emergency food assistance, Food for Peace (FFP).

Table 2. CY2014 International and U.S. Funding, by Destination Country
(As of March 3, 2014)

Destination Country	All Donors, 2014 Contributed/ Committed Funding, as of March 3, 2014[a]	United States, 2014 Contributed/ Committed Funding, as of March 3, 2014[a]	United States Funding as a Percentage of Total Funding
Bulgaria	53,469	$0	0%
Egypt	$7,616,928	$5,300,000	70%
Iraq	$51,080,811	$12,000,000	23%
Jordan	$128,333,778	$35,200,000	27%

Syria: Overview of the Humanitarian Response   113

Destination Country	All Donors, 2014 Contributed/ Committed Funding, as of March 3, 2014[a]	United States, 2014 Contributed/ Committed Funding, as of March 3, 2014[a]	United States Funding as a Percentage of Total Funding
Lebanon	$209,517,175	$38,300,000	18%
Region	$251,549,176	$149,155,172	59%
Syrian Arab Republic	$296,283,130	$159,345,900	54%
Turkey	$14,825,919	$7,644,828	52%
TOTAL	**$959,260,386**	**$406,945,900**	**42%**

Source: Compiled by CRS from information provided by the Financial Tracking Service (FTS) of the United Nations Office for the Coordination of Humanitarian Affairs (OCHA) at http://fts.unocha.org/pageloader.aspx?page=home. Information on the FTS database is self-reported by donor countries and implementing agencies.

a. Contribution: the actual payment of funds or transfer of in-kind goods from the donor to the recipient. Commitment: a legal, contractual obligation between the donor and recipient entity, specifying the amount to be contributed.

Table 3. CY2012-2013 International and U.S. Funding, by Destination Country

Destination Countries	All Donors, 2012-2013 Contributed/ Committed Funding[a]	United States, 2012-2013 Contributed/ Committed Funding[a]	United States Funding as a Percentage of Total Funding
Egypt	$38,630,472	$15,999,210	41%
Iraq	$237,507,737	$67,464,982	28%
Jordan	$1,145,683,191	$190,546,788	17%
Lebanon	$1,134,308,186	$242,381,586	21%
Region	$826,284,839	$77,783,645	9%
Syrian Arab Republic	$1,857,124,558	$671,788,510	36%
Turkey	$260,107,525	$83,416,039	32%
Bulgaria	$1,425,074	$0	0%
Tunisia	$116,897	$0	0%
TOTAL	**$5,501,188,479**	**$1,349,435,759**	**25%**

Source: Compiled by CRS from information provided by the Financial Tracking Service (FTS) of the United Nations Office for the Coordination of Humanitarian Affairs (OCHA) at http://fts.unocha.org/pageloader.aspx?page=home.

Information on the FTS database is self-reported by donor countries and implementing agencies.

a. Contribution: the actual payment of funds or transfer of in-kind goods from the donor to the recipient. Commitment: a legal, contractual obligation between the donor and recipient entity, specifying the amount to be contributed.

Funding for Future Humanitarian Assistance in Syria

The Obama Administration has not elaborated on how it plans to meet future Syria-related needs for the remainder of FY2014. The Administration could continue to draw down global humanitarian accounts, such as MRA or IDA, and if necessary request a supplemental appropriation to replenish them, or use Emergency Refugee and Migration Assistance (ERMA) funds. Possible options could also include reprogramming funds from the Overseas Contingency Operations (OCO) account.[20] The Administration's FY2015 budget request seeks $1.1 billion in humanitarian assistance for Syria and the region. Details of this request include (1) $635 million from the International Disaster Assistance (IDA) Overseas Contingency Operations (OCO) account, of which $335 million would be administered by USAID's Office of Foreign Disaster Assistance (OFDA) and $300 million would be administered by USAID's Office of Food for Peace for emergency assistance, and (2) $465 million from the Migration and Refugee Assistance (MRA) OCO account.[21]

The sharp increase in needs of Syrians affected by the conflict may lead Congress to consider future funding requests from the Administration, including a potential supplemental request, if the situation worsens or persists. It remains to be seen how needs related to the Syria crisis are to be balanced with other humanitarian priorities worldwide, particularly if a major disaster or crisis occurs.

Branding

At points during the conflict, Members of Congress have demonstrated an interest in the labeling or "branding" of U.S. humanitarian aid delivered to Syria so that recipients are aware of its American origins. This issue is complicated in the Syria context. Very little U.S. assistance is currently being branded. The U.S. government is trying to balance the desire to maintain visibility as a contributor of humanitarian assistance with concerns for the security of aid recipients and implementing partners who could become possible targets of attacks. Finding appropriate ways for the United States to leverage its political objectives without politicizing humanitarian aid remains a significant challenge. There has been some debate about whether the United States is receiving adequate political benefit from its humanitarian assistance efforts. Anecdotal evidence from field reports and implementing partners suggests that many Syrians who may be receiving U.S. assistance remain unaware of its origins, or assume it is from a foreign government other than the United States.

In response, some Members of Congress and observers have argued that the United States should begin to more aggressively brand U.S. aid to enhance local perceptions that the people of the United States stand in solidarity with Syrians.[22] Humanitarian groups argue that objectives such as winning hearts and minds potentially compromise the neutrality of humanitarian assistance in general. In the context of Syria, experts contend that if a U.S.-funded clinic were to be targeted for its U.S. affiliation, it could jeopardize much broader humanitarian efforts there. Moreover, it is unclear whether raising awareness of U.S. humanitarian assistance would do much to change perceptions, as Syrians who support the opposition want weapons and other kinds of military help. The Administration is reportedly looking into ways of branding U.S aid that do not jeopardize the safety of those on the ground.

U.N. AND INTERNATIONAL HUMANITARIAN EFFORTS

International efforts to address the humanitarian situation in Syria range from global U.N. appeals to on-the-ground food aid to communities and assistance in camps and settlements. The following sections describe these and other activities in more detail.

International Response Framework

International humanitarian agencies and governments continue to work in Syria and in countries in the region to provide and coordinate assistance to the civilian populations. UNOCHA leads the humanitarian effort within Syria and has established relief sectors—or "clusters"—where possible. UNHCR leads efforts to provide assistance to Syrian refugees in neighboring countries, including non-food items such as shelter, clothing, fuel, cash assistance, and other essential items, as well as assistance to host communities that are supporting refugees.

In Syria, humanitarian access is constrained by a number of factors, including insecurity and conflict, obstruction by the Syrian government or opposition forces, lack of transportation, and limited availability of fuel. The Syrian regime significantly restricts the ability of humanitarian organizations to operate by imposing bureaucratic and administrative obstacles, such as visa restrictions for U.N. staff, international organizations, and NGOs, and limiting the number of humanitarian partnerships. While the Syrian government has permitted some aid deliveries across conflict lines ("cross-line") from Damascus to opposition-held areas using interagency humanitarian convoys, numerous checkpoints are in place en route. Cross-border access to deliver humanitarian assistance from neighboring countries to opposition areas requires the agreement and cooperation of the Syrian authorities.

A number of independent aid agencies are reportedly using a two-track system for aid delivery into Syria. One is through official channels in Damascus, the other through cross-border mechanisms, such as trucking aid through Jordan and Turkey. U.N. agencies are not allowed to work across borders without Syria's consent, unless authorized by the U.N. Security Council. Speaking before the Security Council onApril 18, 2013, ValerieAmos, U.N. Under Secretary General for Humanitarian Affairs and Emergency Relief Coordinator, urged the Council to grant aid agencies cross-border access without the Syrian government's permission. Experts recognize that providing humanitarian assistance within Syria may help to stem the tide of refugees seeking assistance across borders.

In Syria, the United Nations and its partners have identified activities in different sectors that reflect the key priorities. Relief sectors include food security; community services and protection; health; food; water and sanitation; and shelter and non-food items. (For examples of humanitarian activities, see **Appendix B**.)

Organizations operating in-country include the Syrian Arab Red Crescent (SARC), a key Syrian implementing partner with more than 10,000 volunteers.[23] The International Committee of the Red Cross (ICRC), while maintaining its independence as a separate international organization, works with the SARC throughout the country. A number of other organizations are also working on the humanitarian response. These include 10 U.N. agencies, plus the U.N. Department of Safety and Security (UNDSS), the International Organization for Migration (IOM), and 12 international NGOs that have been authorized by the government of Syria to work with SARC. In addition, a

Syria: Overview of the Humanitarian Response 117

handful of other international NGOs have agreements with relevant Syrian ministries. The government of Syria has authorized some national NGOs to provide humanitarian assistance in partnership with the United Nations. U.N. agencies have set up or are in the process of setting up hubs in several locations throughout the country.

The U.N. Relief and Works Agency for Palestine Refugees in the Near East (UNRWA) is also actively responding to the needs of Palestinian refugees affected by the conflict in Syria and those who have fled to other areas within UNRWA's mandate, particularly Jordan and Lebanon. For examples of humanitarian partners working in Syria and neighboring countries, see **Appendix C.**

U.N. Appeals and Other Donor Funding

Donor funding is usually provided in response to a crisis in the form of financial contributions or relief supplies.[24] The Consolidated Appeal Process (CAP), now renamed the Strategic Response Plan (SRP), administered through UNOCHA, brings aid organizations together to coordinate a response to major humanitarian crises and disasters and appeal for funds through a collaborative plan. Funding provided for the Syria humanitarian crisis is in part through two separate U.N. appeals: the Syrian Humanitarian Assistance Response Plan (SHARP) and the Regional Refugee Response Plan (RRP). Contributions to the crisis have also been made outside of the U.N. appeals process.

The SHARP and RRP appeals have been revised several times as the Syria crisis has evolved and humanitarian needs have increased. The December 18, 2012, version of the appeals was the fourth revision and covered the period January to June 2013. The fifth revision of the appeals, covering all of 2013, was launched on June 7, 2013. The sixth revision of the appeals, was launched on December 16, 2013.Together the latest SHARP and RRP appeals total $6.5 billion, making it the largest appeal for a single humanitarian emergency in the history of the United Nations.

As of March 3, 2014, taken together the appeals are 12% funded. See **Appendix D** for a list of the top 25 country donors to the Syria crisis in 2012-2014.

Syria Humanitarian Assistance Response Plan
The Syria Humanitarian Assistance Response Plan (SHARP), which includes U.N. entities and humanitarian partners, is a U.N. appeal seeking $2.3

billion for projects inside Syria from January 1 to December 31, 2014. The plan addresses the needs of Syrians affected by conflict inside Syria. Its priorities include providing relief supplies such as food, healthcare, and water to the most vulnerable; assisting people who have fled their homes and the communities hosting them; and supporting reconstruction of critical infrastructure, including hospitals. The latest revision outlines strategic objectives and builds on findings from sectoral assessments conducted during 2013.

Regional Refugee Response Plan

A second U.N. appeal seeks nearly $4.2 billion for a Regional Refugee Response Plan (RRP) to cover the protection and assistance needs of up to 3.4 million Syrian refugees in the region and covers the period from January 1 to December 31, 2014. The current plan brings together the coordinated efforts of international and national organizations with UNHCR continuing to lead the overall response.[25] The main priorities for the RRP include protection, life-saving assistance, access to basic services, durable solutions (such as resettlement), and community outreach to refugees residing in urban areas and support to host communities.

Contributions Outside the U.N. Appeals

Additional bilateral and other contributions and pledges are also made outside of the U.N. appeals through direct bilateral assistance to governments, international organizations, and NGOs. Some analysts claim that a lack of transparency about these contributions makes it difficult to know what is being funded, where aid may be duplicated, and whether it is being distributed equitably among groups of different ethnic, religious, or political affiliations.

Table 4. CY2014 Requirements and Funding Received for the Syria Humanitarian Assistance Response Plan (SHARP)

Syria Humanitarian Assistance Response Plan (SHARP): January-December 2014			
Revised Requirements	Funding Received[a]	Unmet Requirements	% Funded
$2,276,149,354	$177,387,900	$2,098,761,454	8%

Source: Compiled by CRS using information provided by the Financial Tracking Service.

a. Contributions and commitments received as of March 3, 2014.

Syria: Overview of the Humanitarian Response 119

**Table 5. CY2014 Requirements and Funding
for the Syria Regional Refugee
Response Plan (RRP)**

Syria Regional Refugee Response Plan (RRP): January-December 2014			
Revised Requirements	Funding Received[a]	Unmet Requirements	% Funded
$4,264,717,711	$590,925,181	$3,673,792,530	14%

Source: Compiled by CRS using information provided by the Financial Tracking Service.

a. Contributions and commitments received as of March 3, 2014.

**Table 6. CY2014 Total Requirements and
Funding Received for
Syrian Crisis**

2014 Total Funding to Appeals (SHARP and RRP) and Projects Outside the Appeals						
Revised Requirements for Appeals	Funding Received by Appeals Agencies[a]	Unmet Requirements for Appeals	% Appeals are Funded	Funding Received for Projects Outside the Appeals[a]	Total Funding to the Syria Crisis 2014 (Appeals and Other Projects)[a]
$6,540,867,065	$768,313,081	$5,772,553,984	12%	$190,947,305	$959,260,386

Source: Compiled by CRS using information provided by the Financial Tracking Service.

a. Contributions and commitments received as of March 3, 2014.

In addition, UNOCHA draws on several smaller humanitarian funding sources as follows:

Syria Emergency Response Fund[26]

UNOCHA established the Emergency Response Fund (ERF) for Syria in mid-2012 to support the humanitarian response for the Syria crisis. In CY2012-2013, ERF provided support to local NGOs working in conflict areas in Syria that were difficult to reach. It also provided funding for projects in Jordan, Lebanon, and Iraq.

Central Emergency Response Fund (CERF)

As an international, multilateral funding mechanism, the Central Emergency Response Fund (CERF) aims to focus on early intervention, timely response, and increased capacity and support to underfunded crises. CERF was launched as part of the U.N. reform process in 2006 to strengthen the U.N.'s capacity to respond more efficiently, effectively, and consistently to natural disasters and humanitarian emergencies. It is managed by the Emergency Relief Coordinator and head of UNOCHA. In CY2012-2013, CERF provided funds to a number of appealing agencies in Jordan, Lebanon, and Syria.

Donor Conferences

On January 30, 2013, donors pledged $1.5 billion in humanitarian aid at the International Humanitarian Pledging Conference for Syria, hosted by Kuwait and chaired by U.N. Secretary-General Ban Ki-moon. A portion of the pledges made are helping to fund the SHARP and RRP (U.N. appeals) mentioned above for the humanitarian response in Syria and neighboring countries.

Since then, donors have made other pledges. With the slow pace of funding of these appeals, concerns remain about whether many of the pledges will result in actual contributions.

On September 16, 2013, Sweden hosted a donor conference, organized by UNOCHA, between donors and U.N. representatives to discuss coordination of the humanitarian operation in Syria and its neighboring countries. The forum offered the opportunity to share information and to discuss how to manage the challenges of supplying humanitarian assistance to those affected by the crisis.

On January 15, 2014, Kuwait hosted a second donors conference for Syria, which was chaired by U.N. Secretary General Ban Ki-moon. Donors pledged $2 billion in humanitarian aid. See **Appendix A** for a list of pledges not converted to commitments as of March 3, 2014.

LOOKING AHEAD: KEY CHALLENGES

As Congress considers funding and legislation addressing the humanitarian situation in Syria, Members may want to take a number of challenges and policy issues into account:

Syria: Overview of the Humanitarian Response   121

- **Impeded international humanitarian response.** Despite the provision of substantial humanitarian assistance, insecurity within Syria and lack of cooperation by the Syrian government has severely hampered efforts by governments, U.N. entities, and humanitarian partners to access affected areas to provide humanitarian assistance to populations in need.
- **Funding Shortfalls.** Although the United Nations and governments, including the United States, have worked with both traditional and non-traditional donors to generate and increase contributions, the two U.N. appeals remain underfunded.
- **Willingness and cooperation of neighboring countries.** So far, Jordan, Lebanon, and Turkey have received the vast majority of refugees from Syria. The United States and the international community have recognized the contribution of neighboring countries and supported their efforts while simultaneously encouraging them to keep their borders open to those fleeing the conflict. Nevertheless, in the short term, the increasing numbers of refugees strain the infrastructure and capacity of these countries, and in the long term, they create concerns that the situation could become protracted with limited ongoing international support and attention.
- **Ongoing capacity by the international community to keep pace with humanitarian developments.** The urgent humanitarian needs coupled with the speed at which the situation is changing have many experts concerned that the international response capacity could be overwhelmed if the current pace and scope of conflict and displacement continues.

Amid these factors, Congress may also need to weigh the following:

- **Balancing priorities.** Finding the resources to sustain U.S. aid pledges may be difficult in light of domestic budget constraints. When humanitarian emergencies like the Syria situation require immediate emergency relief, the Administration may fund pledges by depleting most global humanitarian accounts. In order to respond to future humanitarian crises, however, these resources would need to be replenished. If not replenished, U.S. capacity to respond to other emergencies could be diminished.
- **Burdensharing.** Both Congress and the Administration have encouraged other countries to provide humanitarian assistance for the

Syria situation and to turn pledges into actual commitments. It is not always evident whether figures listing donor amounts represent pledges of support or more specific obligations. Pledges made by governments do not always result in actual contributions, as demonstrated by the donor conferences in Kuwait. It also cannot be assumed that the funds committed to relief actually represent new contributions, since the money may have been previously allocated elsewhere. Moreover, it is not readily apparent how the actual costs of a humanitarian emergency might be shared among international donors. Comparing U.S. assistance and international aid can also be difficult because of the often dramatically different forms the assistance takes (relief items versus cash, for instance).

More broadly, political considerations play a role in the way humanitarian assistance is given and to whom. While the images of human suffering only reinforce the need to "do something," humanitarian assistance carries some weight as an instrument of "neutral" intervention and is the most flexible policy tool that can be quickly brought to bear in a crisis. Sometimes humanitarian assistance is expanded beyond its immediate function to avert a crisis, to provide support to allies, and to maintain a presence in the region. How it is used and whether it becomes more of a strategic, policy tool depends upon the situation, what other governments are doing, and the degree to which the United States has further interest in the region.

Providing humanitarian assistance also raises questions about implications for future action. On the one hand, if the United States decides to reduce its humanitarian support to Syria, would this diminish U.S. standing among its allies or affect its interests in other ways?

On the other hand, since the President has a great deal of flexibility over U.S. involvement, once commitment to a humanitarian effort is made, does this make the long-term U.S. participation in reconstruction and political solutions more likely? Regardless, the level and sources of U.S. humanitarian assistance will inevitably have an important impact not only on the Syrian relief operation itself, but on broader U.S. foreign policy goals.

APPENDIX A. SELECTED IMPLEMENTING PARTNERS RECEIVING U.S. FUNDING, CY2014

Implementing Agency	U.S. Funding Received	Projects
United Nations High Commissioner for Refugees (UNHCR)	$104,700,000	Providing protection, camp management, shelter and settlements,water, sanitation, and hygiene services, education, relief commodities, and non-food items to refugees and internally displaced persons in Syria, Jordan, Lebanon, Turkey, Egypt, and Iraq.
World Food Program (WFP)	$107,845,900	Providing emergency food assistance; providing logistics and coordination support to humanitarian operations assisting internally displaced persons (IDPs) in Syria and refugees in host countries.
United Nations Relief and Works Agency for Palestine Refugees in the Near East (UNRWA)	$28,100,000	Throughout the region, providing shelter, food, relief commodities, health, protection, education, and water, sanitation, and hygiene to Palestinian refugees who were living in Syria.
United Nations Children's Fund (UNICEF)	$65,700,000	Maintaining or resuming primary, secondary, and vocational education in Syria; improving access to water, sanitation, and hygiene; protecting children; supporting primary health care services for children and mothers; providing assistance for refugee in all destination countries and for IDPs in Syria.
World Health Organization	$13,000,000	Revitalizing primary health care services and restoring health facilities in Syria.
United Nations Population Fund	$4,200,000	In Syria, providing reproductive health care in affected areas. Throughout the region, providing mental health services, capacity building, and protection.
Food and Agriculture Organization	$1,000,000	Emergency support for crop production in Syria.
United Nations Department of Safety and Security	$500,000	Safety and security for organizations providing humanitarian assistance in Syria.
International Organization for Migration (IOM)	$3,600,000	Supplying relief commodities and border transport in Jordan, Iraq, Lebanon, Turkey, and Egypt.

(Continued)

Implementing Agency	U.S. Funding Received	Projects
International Committee of the Red Cross (ICRC)	$10,800,000	To provide health services, relief commodities, shelter, water, sanitation, and hygiene services, and capacity building throughout the region.
Other U.N. Agencies, NGOs, and other recipients (details not yet provided)	$67,500,000	Providing mental health and psychosocial support services, reproductive health services, livelihood support, capacity building, gender-based violence services, shelter and settlements, case management, humanitarian aid for refugees and internally displaced persons, relief commodities, protection, water, sanitation, and hygiene services, and food assistance throughout the region.

Source: Compiled by CRS from information provided by the Financial Tracking Service (FTS) of the United Nations Office for the Coordination of Humanitarian Affairs (OCHA) at http://fts.unocha.org/pageloader.aspx?page=home. Information on the FTS database is self-reported by donor countries and implementing agencies.

APPENDIX B. SELECTED HUMANITARIAN PROJECTS FUNDED BY ALL DONORS IN SYRIA AND THE REGION

Table B-1. Agencies Implementing Projects within the Syria Humanitarian Assistance Response Plan (SHARP), the Regional Refugee Response Plan (RRP), and Projects Outside the Appeals

Appealing Agency/ Organization	CY2012 Contributions/ Commitments	CY2013 Contributions/ Commitments	CY2014 Contributions/ Commitments, as of March 3, 2014
United Nations High Commissioner for Refugees (UNHCR)	**$199,833,339**	**$947,524,426**	**$327,798,124**
In Syria and the region, UNHCR provides shelter and basic non-food items, protection in camps and settlements, education services, and water, sanitation, and hygiene services. UNHCR is also meeting the urgent basic needs of flood-affected refugees in Za'atri camp in Jordan.			

Syria: Overview of the Humanitarian Response

Appealing Agency/ Organization	CY2012 Contributions/ Commitments	CY2013 Contributions/ Commitments	CY2014 Contributions/ Commitments, as of March 3, 2014
World Food Program (WFP)	**$193,817,890**	**$854,822,450**	**$174,615,672**
Within Syria and the refugee destination countries, the WFP provides emergency food assistance; logistics and telecommunications coordination to support humanitarian operations; security for humanitarian organizations; and armored vehicles for WFP personnel.			
United Nations Children's Fund (UNICEF)	**$89,961,837**	**$487,961,926**	**$104,834,300**
UNICEF projects include humanitarian response activities in Jordan, Lebanon, Turkey, and Iraq, including the provision of Water, Sanitation, and Hygiene services (WASH) in refugee communities and shelters for internally displaced persons; the continuation of education of Syrian children in Lebanon; the resumption of education programs in Syria; the provision of basic health care for children; the provision of child-friendly spaces and psycho-social support at school and in communities; food aid and immunization programs for children; child protection services in refugee communities; winter blankets; armored vehicles for safety and security for humanitarian staff.			
United Nations Relief and Works Agency for Palestine Refugees in the Near East (UNRWA)	**$29,180,912**	**$225,648,117**	**$66,410,660**
In Syria and the region, UNRWA projects provide food and non-food assistance to Palestinian refugees who are living in Syria or who have taken refuge in neighboring countries. UNRWA provides emergency shelter; emergency medical supplies and health services; emergency cash assistance; access to clean water; emergency hospital care; armored vehicles for safety of humanitarian workers; Water, Sanitation, and Hygiene (WASH) projects; shelter; emergency education; protection.			
World Health Organization (WHO)	**$12,189,628**	**$95,121,342**	**$30,563,678**
WHO provides operational support for health interventions; offers critical medical assistance, including trauma services; fills gaps in basic health care; fills supply gaps for management of chronic illnesses; expands nutritional support services; provides essential medicines and medical equipment for operating theaters and lifesaving surgeries; and primary health care services for persons in Syria and refugee destination countries.			

Table B-1. (Continued)

Appealing Agency/ Organization	CY2012 Contributions/ Commitments	CY2013 Contributions/ Commitments	CY2014 Contributions/ Commitments, as of March 3, 2014
Emergency Response Fund (United Nations Office for the Coordination of Humanitarian Affairs UNOCHA)	$19,826,503	$23,113,659	$15,704,209
The Emergency Response Fund for Syria mobilizes and channels resources to humanitarian partners so they may respond to the crisis in Syria and initiate life-saving humanitarian activities in Syria and neighboring countries.			
United Nations Population Fund (UNFPA)	$3,356,698	$28,554,137	$11,179,261
In Syria and the refugee-destination countries, UNFPA projects provide the following: emergency reproductive health kits; pharmaceuticals to hosts of refugee communities; reproductive health care, focusing on at-risk pregnancies and other life-threatening conditions; gender-based violence prevention and response; emergency support to refugee women and girls; mental health care; protection.			
International Committee of the Red Cross	$65,426,131	$144,189,188	$24,950,212
In Syria and the refugee destination countries, the ICRC is providing emergency health and medical assistance, protection, shelter, WASH services, and protection activities.			
Danish Refugee Council	$15,393,127	$97,948,119	$2,165,000
The Danish Refugee Council provides emergency shelter assistance and non-food items to displaced persons in Syria. It also provides cash assistance, clothing and blankets, and emergency assistance to refugees in the region.			
Norwegian Refugee Council	$12,212,823	$25,658,251	$26,727,325
The Norwegian Refugee Council provides refugees in Lebanon and Jordan with helter and protection support.			
Save the Children	$6,529,048	$58,757,357	$7,941,234
Save the Children provides refugees in the region with protection, psychosocial services, shelter kits, vouchers for clothing and cash assistance, and education services.			
Agency for Technical Cooperation and	$2,366,711	$9,233,637	$6,114,130

Syria: Overview of the Humanitarian Response 127

Development (ACTED)			
Appealing Agency/ Organization	CY2012 Contributions/ Commitments	CY2013 Contributions/ Commitments	CY2014 Contributions/ Commitments, as of March 3, 2014
In Lebanon, ACTED provides refugees with hygiene kits and storage containers for water, constructs/rehabilitates water networks, and constructs/rehabilitates latrines. In Jordan, ACTED assesses and provides health, psycho-social, legal, education, and family tracing services for children at risk or unaccompanied children. ACTED also renovates and refurbishes schools for refugee children, provides cash assistance, upgrades sub-standard shelters, and provides safe access to drinking water, toilets, and soap. In Iraq, ACTED provides work opportunities for refugees.			
International Organization for Migration (IOM)	$7,891,570	$75,711,851	$8,034,698
IOM provides IDPs in Syria and refugees who have gone to neighboring countries with emergency shelter materials, non-food items, emergency healthcare, livelihood support, and transport assistance to camps and settlements.			
Mercy Corps.	$1,693,701	$54,025,774	$0
Mercy Corps is integrating Syrian and Iraqi refugee children with disabilities into Jordan's public schools. In Lebanon, Mercy Corps provides protection, non-food items, and WASH services for refugees.			
Islamic Relief Worldwide	$1,010,418	$24,545,950	$0
Islamic Relief Worldwide provides food, subsidies for rent, non-food items, and hygiene kits to Syrian refugees in the host countries. Islamic Relief also provides medical aid inside Syria.			
Other Appealing Agencies and Organizations	$339,273,693	$1,348,408,266	$152,221,883
TOTAL All Appealing Agencies and Organizations	$999,964,029	$4,501,224,450	$959,260,386

Source: Compiled by CRS from information provided by the Financial Tracking Service (FTS) of the United Nations Office for the Coordination of Humanitarian Affairs (OCHA) at http://fts.unocha.org/pageloader.aspx?page=home. Information on the FTS database is self-reported by donor countries and implementing agencies.

APPENDIX C. SELECTED HUMANITARIAN PARTNERS SERVING THE SYRIA ARAB REPUBLIC CIVIL UNREST, CY2014

ACT Alliance/ DanChurchAid and	Action Contre la Faim (ACF)	Agency for Technical Cooperation and Development
ACT Alliance/Lutheran World Federation		
Al Mamoura	CARITAS	LOVEK V T SNI
Danish Red Cross	Danish Refugee Council	Diakonie Katastrophenhilfe
Emergency Response Fund (OCHA)	Foundation Caritas Luxembourg	Food & Agriculture Organization of the United Nations (FAO)
Gruppo Volontariato Civile	Handicap International	Humedica
International Committee of the Red Cross(ICRC)	International Federation of Red Cross and Red Crescent Societies	International Medical Corps
International Organization for Migration(IOM)	International Rescue Committee	Japan Emergency NGO
Les Sarments de Lavaux	Malteser International	Médecins du Monde
Nippon International Cooperation for Community Development	Norwegian Refugee Council	Office for the Coordination of Humanitarian Affairs (OCHA)
OXFAM	Red Crescent Society of the United Arab Emirates	RedR
Save the Children	United Nations Children's Fund (UNICEF)	United Nations Department of Safety and Security
United Nations Development Program	United Nations Entity for Gender Equality and the Empowerment of Women	United Nations High Commissioner for Refugees (UNHCR)

United Nations Industrial Development Organization	United Nations Population Fund (UNFPA)	United Nations Relief and Works Agency for Palestine Refugees in the Near East
World Food Program	World Health Organization (WHO)	World Vision International

Source: Compiled by CRS from information provided by the Financial Tracking Service (FTS) of the United Nations Office for the Coordination of Humanitarian Affairs (OCHA) at http://fts.unocha.org/pageloader.aspx?page=home. Information on the FTS database is self-reported by donor countries and implementing agencies.

APPENDIX D. U.S. AND INTERNATIONAL HUMANITARIAN COUNTRY DONORS TO THE SYRIA CRISIS, CY2012-2014

Table D-1. Top 25 Country Donors in Response to the Syria Arab Republic Civil Unrest Humanitarian Funding

(U.S. $)				
Donor Countries	**CY2012 Contributed/ Committed Funding[a]**	**CY2013 Contributed/ Committed Funding**	**CY2014 Contributed/ Committed Funding, as of March 3, 2014**	**CY2012-2014 Funding Totals, as of March 3, 2014**
United States	$207,402,281	$1,142,033,478	$406,945,900	$1,756,381,659[b]
European Commission	$107,028,800	$602,685,889	$200,190,728	$909,905,417
United Kingdom	$79,942,823	$438,773,283	$169,226,572	$687,942,678
Germany	$99,291,127	$333,267,430	$23,531,571	$456,090,128
Kuwait	$8,163,142	$325,057,835	$0	$333,220,977

Table D-1. (Continued)

Donor Countries	CY2012 Contributed/ Committed Funding[a]	CY2013 Contributed/ Committed Funding	CY2014 Contributed/ Committed Funding, as of March 3, 2014	CY2012-2014 Funding Totals, as of March 3, 2014
Canada	$23,382,589	$180,016,204	$0	$203,398,793
Japan	$14,260,875	$122,467,701	$52,487,438	$189,216,014
Saudi Arabia	$65,904,507	$90,699,774	$17,968,880	$174,573,161
Norway	$26,077,908	$75,924,186	$24,254,977	$126,257,071
Qatar	$50,846,902	$66,237,898	$0	$117,084,800
Australia	$29,339,428	$71,804,647	$8,915,892	$110,059,967
United Arab Emirates	$14,364,202	$85,740,666	$2,626,583	$102,731,451
Denmark	$11,372,872	$58,184,530	$13,967,517	$83,524,919
Sweden	$25,977,007	$56,181,917	$0	$82,158,924
Netherlands	$30,028,753	$46,285,249	$1,595,755	$77,909,757
Switzerland	$16,935,268	$42,707,782	$551,268	$60,194,318
France	$20,503,584	$27,296,968	$0	$47,800,552
Italy	$9,123,610	$27,172,219	$155,459	$36,451,288
Finland	$4,617,223	$22,936,064	$0	$27,553,287
Russian Federation	$9,500,000	$14,800,000	$1,000,000	$25,300,000
Belgium	$2,973,897	$17,723,670	$2,758,621	$23,456,188
Ireland	$2,870,464	$15,710,182	$0	$18,580,646
Spain	$2,184,087	$12,394,481	$0	$14,578,568
China	$6,702,932	$3,200,000	$3,900,000	$13,802,932
Austria	$3,908,941	$6,990,277	$63,859	$10,963,077

Donor Countries	CY2012 Contributed/ Committed Funding[a]	CY2013 Contributed/ Committed Funding	CY2014 Contributed/ Committed Funding, as of March 3, 2014	CY2012-2014 Funding Totals, as of March 3, 2014
TOTAL Top 25 Country Donors	$872,703,222	$3,886,292,330	$930,141,020	$5,689,136,572
Private (individuals and organizations)	$18,368,940	$325,768,162	$8,349,715	$352,486,817
TOTAL Other Country Donors, NGOs, and other Organizations	$108,891,867	$289,163,958	$20,769,651	$418,825,476
TOTAL All Donors	$999,964,029	$4,501,224,450	$959,260,386	$6,460,448,865

Source: Compiled by CRS from information provided by the Financial Tracking Service (FTS) of the United Nations Office for the Coordination of Humanitarian Affairs (OCHA) at http://fts.unocha.org/pageloader.aspx?page=home. Information on the FTS database is self-reported by donor countries and implementing agencies.

a. Contribution: the actual payment of funds or transfer of in-kind goods from the donor to the recipient. Commitment: a legal, contractual obligation between the donor and recipient entity, specifying the amount to be contributed.

b. The U.S. funding total in **Appendix D** differs from the amount in the USAID, "Syria-Complex Emergency" Fact Sheet #10, Fiscal Year (FY) 2014, March 13, 2014. This discrepancy has not been reconciled.

APPENDIX E. 2013 PLEDGES NOT CONVERTED TO COMMITMENTS OR CONTRIBUTIONS AS OF SEPTEMBER 11, 2013

Table E-1. Pledges Not Converted

Donor	Date of Pledge[a]	Amount Pledged	Outstanding pledge as of March 3, 2014
Australia	January 15, 2014	$8,912,656	$0
Belgium	January 15, 2014	$7,558,480	$4,754,198
Botswana	January 15, 2014	$50,000	$50,000
Brazil	January 15, 2014	$300,000	$300,000
Bulgaria	January 15, 2014	$137,931	$137,931
Canada	January 24, 2014	$150,000,000	$150,000,000
Croatia	January 15, 2014	$206,897	$206,897
Cyprus	January 15, 2014	$13,793	$13,793
Czech Republic	January 15, 2014	$1,379,310	$1,379,310
Denmark	January 15, 2014	$37,000,000	$22,986,252
Estonia	January 15, 2014	$551,724	$275,862
European Commission	January 15, 2014	$225,000,000	$225,000,000
Finland	January 15, 2014	$9,655,172	$9,655,172
France	January 15, 2014	$27,586,207	$27,586,207
Germany	January 15, 2014	$110,000,000	$105,585,257
Hungary	January 15, 2014	$137,931	$137,931
India	January 15, 2014	$2,000,000	$2,000,000
Iraq	January 15, 2014	$13,000,000	$13,000,000
Ireland	January 15, 2014	$16,551,724	$16,551,724
Italy	January 15, 2014	$51,300,000	$51,300,000
Japan	January 15, 2014	$120,000,000	$67,512,562
Korea, Republic of	January 15, 2014	$5,000,000	$5,000,000
Kuwait	January 15, 2014	$500,000,000	$500,000,000
Luxembourg	January 15, 2014	$6,896,552	$6,896,552
Malaysia	January 15, 2014	$500,000	$500,000
Mexico	January 15, 2014	$3,000,000	$2,000,000
Netherlands	January 15, 2014	$17,931,035	$17,931,035
New Zealand	January 15, 2014	$4,095,004	$4,095,004
NGO Consortium	January 15, 2014	$207,000,000	$207,000,000
Norway	January 15, 2014	$75,200,262	$75,200,262

Syria: Overview of the Humanitarian Response 133

Donor	Date of Pledge[a]	Amount Pledged	Outstanding pledge as of March 3, 2014
Oman	January 15, 2014	$10,000,000	$10,000,000
Poland	January 15, 2014	$800,000	$800,000
Qatar	January 15, 2014	$60,000,000	$60,000,000
Romania	January 15, 2014	$100,000	$100,000
Saudi Arabia	January 15, 2014	$60,000,000	$56,387,483
Slovakia	January 15, 2014	$137,931	$97,255
Spain	January 15, 2014	$7,586,207	$7,586,207
Sweden	January 15, 2014	$35,298,629	$35,298,629
Switzerland	January 15, 2014	$33,821,871	$33,821,871
United Arab Emirates	January 15, 2014	$60,000,000	$60,000,000
United Kingdom	January 15, 2014	$164,000,000	$0
United States	January 15, 2014	$380,000,000	$0
TOTAL PLEDGES		**$2,412,709,316**	**$1,781,147,394**

Source: Compiled by CRS from information provided by the Financial Tracking Service (FTS) of the United Nations Office for the Coordination of Humanitarian Affairs (OCHA) at http://fts.unocha.org/pageloader.aspx?page=home. Information on the FTS database is self-reported by donor countries and implementing agencies.

Notes: *Contribution*: the actual payment of funds or transfer of in-kind goods from the donor to the recipient. *Commitment*: a legal, contractual obligation between the donor and recipient entity, specifying the amount to be contributed

a. Pledge: a non-binding announcement of an intended contribution or allocation by the donor.

End Notes

[1] For background on the Syria situation, see CRS Report RL33487, *Armed Conflict in Syria: Overview and U.S. Response*, coordinated by Christopher M. Blanchard.

[2] CRS Report R43201, *Possible U.S. Intervention in Syria: Issues for Congress*, coordinated by Christopher M. Blanchard and Jeremy M. Sharp. See also CRS Report R42848, *Syria's Chemical Weapons: Issues for Congress*, coordinated by Mary Beth D. Nikitin.

[3] The very nature of humanitarian emergencies—the need to respond quickly in order to save lives and provide relief— has resulted in a broad definition of humanitarian assistance, on both a policy and operational level. While humanitarian assistance is assumed to address urgent food, shelter, and medical needs, the agencies within the U.S. government providing this support expand or contract the definition in response to circumstances.

[4] On January 2, 2013, the U.N. Human Rights Office reported individuals killed in Syria between March 15, 2011, and November 30, 2012, numbered 60,000. The figure did not distinguish

between combatants and non-combatants. Navi Pillay, the U.N. Human Rights Commissioner, stressed the analysis was a work in progress. See http://www.ohchr.org/EN/NewsEvents/Pages/DisplayNews.aspx?NewsID=12912&LangID=E. Seven independent groups reportedly contributed to the data analysis, which caused some to question the integrity of the results. The United Nations and others have since cited the 60,000 number as a base figure and added to it over time; for example, subsequent figures cited are 80,000 and then in July 2013, 100,000. An updated study conducted by data specialists on behalf of the Office of the U.N. High Commissioner for Human Rights reported 92,901 documented cases of individuals killed in Syria between March 2011 and the end of April 2013. It remains unclear how many of these casualties are civilian. See "Updated Statistical Analysis of Documentation of Killings in the Syrian Arab Republic," Commissioned by the Office of the U.N. High Commissioner for Human Rights, Human Rights Data Analysis Group, June 13, 2013.

[5] Report of Commission of Inquiry on Syria A/HRC/22/59, February 5, 2013.

[6] For the latest State Department country report see 2013 Country Reports on Human Rights Practices.

[7] Human Rights Council, Resolution S-17/1.

[8] See Overview: http://www.ohchr.org/EN/HRBodies/HRC/IICISyria/Pages/AboutCoI.aspx; and Commission Homepage and Documents (including reports issues by the Commission): http://www.ohchr.org/EN/HRBodies/HRC/IICISyria/Pages/IndependentInternational Commission.aspx.

[9] See U.N. Security Council, Statement by the President of the Security Council, S/PRST/2013/15, October 2, 2013.

[10] OCHA, "Humanitarian Bulletin, Syrian Arab Republic" Issue 41, January 31, 2014.

[11] Office of the Spokesperson for the Secretary-General, Highlights of the Noon Briefing by Farhan Haq, Acting Deputy Spokesperson for the Secretary-General, "U.N. Welcomes Reported Agreement on Humanitarian Pause for Homs, Syria," February 6, 2014.

[12] U.N. Security Council S/RES/2139 (2014), February 22, 2014.

[13] U.N. Security Council S/PRST/2013/15, October 2, 2013.

[14] Secretary-General SG/SM/15665 GA/11486 IHA/1336 "Secretary-General, in General Assembly, Urges Syrian Parties to Ease Humanitarian Access, Treat Civilians Humanely," February 25, 2014.

[15] U.N. Office for the Coordination of Humanitarian Affairs, "Humanitarian Bulletin: Syria," Issue 36, 8 October–4 November 2013.

[16] Registration of refugees is a key step to ensure individuals have access to services and assistance. With the large number of refugees seeking assistance in neighboring countries, the U.N. High Commissioner for Refugees (UNHCR) cannot immediately register all those who seek asylum. Those who approach UNHCR and cannot be registered are given appointments and are considered to be "awaiting registration." Only the more vulnerable individuals receive assistance while waiting to be registered. UNHCR is trying to increase registration capacity and reduce waiting periods in countries hosting Syrian refugees.

[17] For example, several bills in the 113th Congress include provisions that address humanitarian issues, such as H.R. 1327, the Free Syria Act of 2013; S. 617, the Syria Democratic Transition Act of 2013, and S. 960, Syria Transition Support Act of 2013; and hearings, including the Senate Committee on Foreign Relations, "Syria's Humanitarian Crisis," March 19, 2013, the U.S. Helsinki Commission, "Fleeing to Live: Syrian Refugees in the OSCE Region," June 13, 2013; the Senate Committee on Foreign Relations, "Syria Hearing," October 31, 2013.

[18] According to the State Department, there has only been one account transfer to address humanitarian needs. On April 5, 2013, the State Department notified Congress of its intent to reprogram $220 million originally appropriated to the FY2012 Pakistan Counterinsurgency Capability Funds to the humanitarian crisis in Syria. This would include

Syria: Overview of the Humanitarian Response   135

$120 million for the International Disaster Assistance (IDA) account and $100 million for the Migration Refugee Assistance (MRA) account.

[19] The appeals process brings aid organizations together to coordinate a response and appeal for funds through a collaborative plan. The two U.N. appeals, the Syria Humanitarian Assistance Response Plan and the Regional Response Plan, are described in the next section, "U.N. and International Humanitarian Efforts."

[20] Funding for OCO supports "extraordinary, but temporary, costs of the Department of State and USAID in Iraq, Afghanistan, and Pakistan. See Executive Budget Summary, Function 150 & Other International Programs, Fiscal Year 2014, and p. 97.

[21] For the first time in FY2015, the Administration is requesting OCO funds for "ongoing challenges presented by the Syria crisis" and to fund new peacekeeping missions in Africa. Congressional Budget Justification FY2015.

[22] See USAID, "Syria–Complex Emergency," Fact Sheet #10 FY2013, February 28, 2013. Sly, Liz, "U.S. Feeds Syrians, But Discreetly: Humanitarian Aid Operation Shrouded in Secrecy to Protect Recipients and Delivery Staff," *Washington Post*, April 15, 2013, p. 1.

[23] The International Red Cross and Red Crescent Movement is a humanitarian network that provides protection and assistance to people affected by conflict and disasters. The Movement is not a single organization. It has three main components, all of which are guided by seven fundamental principles, including impartiality and neutrality: The International Committee of the Red Cross (ICRC), the International Federation of Red Cross and Red Crescent Societies (IFRC), and 188 individual national Red Cross and Red Crescent Societies, of which SARC is one.

[24] Funding numbers are fluid and subject to change. A full accounting is typically not possible for any crisis. This may be for a variety of reasons: some assistance is not reported to governments and coordinating agencies; there may be delays in recording; and in-kind contributions can be difficult to value (this is typically left to the donor country or organization and can lead to differing standards and lack of consistency across sectors).

[25] Palestinian Refugees are mostly covered under support provided through UNRWA.

[26] Emergency Response Funds (ERF), established in 20 countries since 1997, provide NGOs and U.N. agencies rapid and flexible funding to address gaps in humanitarian response through small grants.

INDEX

A

access, ix, 37, 52, 53, 79, 88, 91, 100, 101, 102, 103, 104, 105, 106, 107, 116, 118, 121, 123, 125, 127, 134
accommodation(s), 32, 107, 108
accountability, 36
accounting, 135
ACF, 128
adverse weather, 83
advisory body, 3
advocacy, 39
Afghanistan, 40, 107, 135
Africa, 111, 135
age, 10
agencies, 37, 105, 113, 114, 115, 116, 120, 124, 127, 129, 131, 133, 135
Air Force, 53
Al Qaeda, viii, 1, 10, 15, 17, 61, 70, 74, 75, 78, 88, 92
Algeria, 111
ambassadors, 45
Anbar Province, viii, 1, 10, 17, 30, 31, 50, 62
anti-Asad forces, viii, 66, 70
anti-government forces, viii, 66, 68
anti-government insurgents, vii, viii, 65, 67
appointments, 134
appropriations, 58
Arab world, 2, 40

Arabian Peninsula, 16
architect, 13
armed conflict, vii
armed forces, 66, 69, 70
armed groups, 9, 15, 28, 68, 69, 70, 73, 74, 76, 89, 93, 96, 103
arms sales, 2, 48, 51
arrest, 25, 30, 36, 42
assassination, 4, 25
assault, 16, 30
assessment, 8, 36, 52
asylum, 101, 134
atrocities, 103
attitudes, 38
Austria, 130
authority(s), 3, 6, 16, 28, 36, 40, 41, 48, 74, 86, 89, 90, 104, 105, 116
autonomy, 19, 20, 25, 44, 67
awareness, 115

B

Baghdad government, vii, 1, 2
Bahrain, 46, 53
banking, 42
base, 41, 134
basic needs, 109, 124
basic services, 118
batteries, 50
battlefield, viii, 66, 68

138 Index

Belgium, 130, 132
benchmarks, 8, 9
benefits, 91
bilateral relationship, 54, 55
blame, 39
blood, 69
Botswana, 132
Brazil, 132
brutality, 66, 70, 74
Bulgaria, 112, 113, 132
businesses, 27

C

calculus, 91
candidates, 7, 10, 11, 12, 13, 18, 24, 29, 34, 77, 96
CAP, 117
capacity building, 123, 124
cash, 115, 122, 125, 126, 127
categorization, 20
ceasefire, 105
certification, 13
challenges, 88, 107, 108, 109, 120, 135
chemical(s), ix, 10, 41, 50, 66, 67, 77, 81, 82, 83, 84, 85, 92, 97, 99, 102, 103
child protection, 125
children, 102, 107, 123, 125, 127
China, 35, 130
Chinese firms, 35
Christians, 39
chronic illness, 125
CIA, 51, 63, 75, 96, 98
city(s), viii, ix, 1, 16, 26, 27, 30, 31, 32, 38, 45, 47, 67, 100, 105, 106, 108
citizens, 31
civil law, 6
civil society, 8, 36, 89
civil war, ix, 28, 66, 72, 81, 100, 101, 105
Civil War, 63
closure, 37
clothing, 103, 115, 126
clusters, 115
collective bargaining, 38
commercial, 21, 83

communication, 91
community(s), 3, 9, 24, 28, 32, 39, 41, 47, 68, 70, 72, 75, 83, 84, 89, 93, 101, 103, 104, 109, 112, 115, 116, 118, 121, 125, 126
community service, 116
competition, 97, 109
competitors, 12
compliance, 56, 106
complications, 73
composition, 5, 61, 74, 93
compounds, 82
conference, 26, 61, 86, 120
conflict, vii, viii, 3, 17, 21, 28, 30, 38, 41, 52, 55, 65, 66, 67, 68, 70, 72, 75, 79, 85, 86, 87, 89, 91, 93, 97, 99, 102, 103, 104, 105, 106, 107, 108, 109, 114, 116, 117, 118, 119, 121, 135
conflict resolution, 55
confrontation, 19, 39, 73
Congress, 1, 2, 5, 12, 16, 20, 31, 49, 50, 60, 65, 66, 67, 68, 72, 85, 86, 89, 90, 92, 99, 101, 110, 114, 115, 120, 121, 133, 134
consensus, 47, 60, 63
consent, 25, 69, 116
Consolidated Appropriations Act, 39, 66, 89
Constitution, 13, 22
construction, 43, 109
containers, 82, 127
contingency, 86, 89, 101, 110
controversial, 102
convention, 9
conversations, 62, 63
cooperation, 3, 19, 35, 42, 49, 51, 52, 53, 54, 66, 83, 92, 97, 101, 116, 121
coordination, viii, 66, 68, 86, 89, 120, 123, 125
corruption, 10, 25, 36, 37, 55, 60
cost, 29, 31, 49, 50, 55
counterterrorism, 32, 51, 53, 55, 77
covering, 117
crimes, 103, 104
crises, 33, 66, 72, 120
critical infrastructure, 118
criticism, 43, 90

Index

139

Croatia, 132
crop, 123
crop production, 123
CT, 32
culture, 36
customers, 35, 42
Cyprus, 132
Czech Republic, 132

D

data analysis, 134
database, 113, 114, 124, 127, 129, 131, 133
deaths, 18
decision makers, 92
defamation, 37
deficiencies, 36, 47
delegates, 67
democracy, 33, 48, 54, 55, 60, 74, 77, 88
Democratic Party, 4, 19, 42
demonstrations, 26
denial, 36
Denmark, 84, 130, 132
Department of Defense, 32, 84, 98
Department of the Treasury, 97
destruction, 81, 82, 83, 84, 92, 97, 106
detainees, 103
detention, 106
developed nations, 54
development assistance, 101
diplomatic efforts, ix, 67, 76, 99
disaster, 72, 114
discrimination, vii, 1, 13, 26, 104
dismantlement, 15
displaced persons, ix, 99, 108, 126
displacement, 103, 106, 121
disposition, 90
distribution, 107, 112
diversification, 93
Doha, 98
dominance, 10
donor countries, 113, 114, 124, 127, 129, 131, 133
donors, 86, 101, 117, 120, 121, 122
draft, 6, 9, 10

drinking water, 127
due process, 37
durability, 9

E

economic boom, 35
economic development, 54, 89
economic progress, 35
economic resources, 3
education, 6, 52, 123, 124, 125, 126, 127
effluents, 97
Egypt, ix, 53, 96, 99, 107, 108, 111, 112, 113, 123
election, 4, 5, 10, 11, 13, 15, 24, 29, 30, 32, 33, 34, 61, 77, 96
electricity, 54
embargo, 56
embassy, 45, 55
emergency, 86, 89, 90, 100, 101, 102, 112, 114, 117, 121, 122, 123, 125, 126, 127
emergency relief, 121
employees, 56
employers, 38
employment, 18
energy, 6, 14, 22, 23, 33, 34, 35, 42, 44, 45, 108
environment, 66, 77, 108
equipment, 2, 31, 32, 49, 50, 52, 74, 82, 83, 88, 90, 93, 125
Estonia, 132
ethnic groups, 9, 21
Europe, 45
European Commission, 129, 132
evidence, 46, 115
evolution, 86
exclusion, 12
executive branch, 38
Executive Order, 18
exercise, 36, 53
exile, 4, 5, 11, 77
expertise, 41, 85
exploitation, 104
export routes, 22, 23
exporter, 55

140   Index

exports, 22, 23, 34, 35, 42, 45
extradition, 45
extremists, 10, 70, 75, 85, 88, 91, 98

F

Facebook, 98
Fallujah, viii, 1, 10, 30, 31, 32
families, 6
family members, 6
family relationships, 37
fear(s), 22, 41, 44, 46, 47, 85, 108
Federal Bureau of Investigation, 75
financial, 9, 32, 42, 80, 84, 92, 117
financial resources, 9, 32
financial sector, 42
Finland, 83, 130, 132
flexibility, 122
flight(s), 43, 107
fluid, ix, 99, 107, 135
food, 81, 91, 103, 105, 106, 107, 112, 115,
    116, 118, 123, 124, 125, 126, 127, 133
food security, 116
force, 2, 3, 20, 27, 33, 39, 40, 43, 46, 47, 48,
    51, 53, 67, 88, 98
foreign aid, 102
foreign allies, vii, viii, 65, 67
foreign exchange, 35
foreign firms, 35
foreign policy, 41, 97, 122
formation, 6, 33, 73, 74
formula, 7
France, 23, 63, 95, 96, 98, 130, 132
freedom, 37, 38, 39
funding, viii, 30, 39, 55, 65, 66, 69, 72, 75,
    84, 86, 87, 88, 89, 93, 100, 102, 112,
    114, 117, 119, 120, 131, 135
funds, 49, 51, 55, 72, 86, 87, 89, 113, 114,
    117, 120, 122, 131, 133, 135

G

GDP, 35
Geneva II, ix, 43, 67, 68, 73, 77, 98, 99, 105

Germany, 24, 26, 84, 96, 129, 132
gestures, 28
global security, 97
God, 73, 75
governance, vii, 3, 5, 9, 60, 89, 91
government funds, 9, 38
government leaders, ix, 99, 105
government ranks, viii, 66, 68
governments, 9, 28, 66, 67, 72, 109, 115,
    118, 121, 122, 135
governor, 9, 29, 30
grants, 9, 135
Grievances, 15
grouping, 30
growth, 7, 12, 35, 66, 72

H

harassment, 37
HCC, 54
health, 24, 82, 104, 106, 116, 123, 124, 125,
    126, 127
health care, 123, 125, 126
health services, 124, 125
height, 28, 39
Hezbollah, 18, 42, 72, 79, 80, 96, 97
history, 19, 41, 100, 117
homeland security, 75
homes, 31, 107, 118
host, 101, 105, 109, 112, 116, 118, 123, 127
hostilities, 103
House, 31, 45, 47, 53, 62, 75, 95, 96
housing, 11, 106
human, vii, 36, 37, 39, 40, 55, 89, 103, 104,
    105, 122
human right(s), vii, 36, 37, 39, 40, 55, 89,
    103, 104, 105
humanitarian aid, 114, 120, 124
humanitarian assistance, viii, 65, 72, 86, 87,
    88, 96, 100, 102, 103, 106, 107, 109,
    110, 111, 112, 114, 115, 116, 117, 120,
    121, 122, 123, 133
humanitarian crises, vii, viii, 99, 117, 121
humanitarian organizations, 100, 101, 102,
    116, 125

Index

humanitarian response, vii, 87, 100, 101, 102, 110, 116, 119, 120, 121, 125, 135
Hungary, 132
hydrolysis, 82
hygiene, 123, 124, 127

I

identity, 74, 88
ideology, 73, 74
image(s), 11, 85, 122
imagery, 93
immigration, 20
immunity, 92
immunization, 103, 125
impact assessment, 82
imprisonment, 37
in transition, 91
independence, 4, 20, 44, 67, 116
India, 132
individuals, 12, 13, 73, 75, 88, 93, 131, 133, 134
Indonesia, 107
industry, 59
infrastructure, 35, 104, 106, 121
insecurity, 116, 121
inspections, 43
inspectors, 67, 84
institutions, 22, 33, 36, 37, 54, 69, 91
insurgency, 15, 16, 17, 32, 70, 95, 98
insurgent challenge, vii, 1
integration, 17
integrity, 39, 73, 134
intelligence, 25, 51, 52, 68, 70, 72, 75, 80
intelligence estimates, 70
interference, 36, 37, 41, 45, 73
internally displaced, viii, 65, 72, 87, 107, 123, 124, 125
International Energy Agency, 35
international law, 103
International Medical Corps, 128
International Narcotics Control, 87
International Rescue Committee, 128
international standards, 37, 55

intervention, viii, 2, 14, 17, 38, 80, 85, 102, 120, 122
intimidation, 37, 39
investment, 35, 56, 66
investors, 34, 35
Iran, 2, 4, 5, 8, 10, 18, 19, 35, 40, 41, 42, 44, 50, 54, 62, 63, 66, 67, 72, 79, 80, 96, 97
Iran Sanctions Act, 44
Iraqi Security Forces, viii, 2, 17, 59
Ireland, 130, 132
ISF, viii, 2, 8, 16, 17, 19, 21, 27, 28, 30, 31, 32, 47, 51, 52, 53, 58, 59
Islam, 6, 75, 96, 98
Islamic law, 6, 38, 66, 67, 70
Islamic state, viii, 1, 15, 16, 66, 70, 73, 74, 75, 88, 92, 96
Israel, 79, 97
issues, vii, 1, 6, 14, 15, 20, 36, 40, 46, 52, 54, 55, 62, 77, 104, 134
Italy, 84, 96, 130, 132

J

Japan, 128, 130, 132
jihad, 75
jihadist, 44
Jordan, ix, 16, 17, 32, 45, 53, 90, 96, 99, 107, 108, 109, 111, 112, 113, 116, 117, 119, 120, 121, 123, 124, 125, 126, 127
journalists, 31, 37
justification, 8, 19, 55

K

Korea, 132
Kurd(s), vii, 1, 6, 7, 8, 9, 10, 19, 20, 21, 22, 23, 24, 30, 32, 39, 42, 44, 50, 57, 60, 62
Kurdish region, vii, 1, 6, 24
Kuwait, 2, 3, 4, 19, 40, 45, 46, 48, 53, 56, 120, 122, 129, 132

L

labeling, 114

landscape, 24
law enforcement, 36
laws, 9, 11, 14, 26, 28, 34, 35, 37, 48
lead, 51, 55, 85, 114, 118, 135
leadership, 11, 13, 21, 24, 27, 40, 43, 55, 56, 73, 91
Lebanon, viii, ix, 42, 43, 52, 66, 72, 79, 80, 97, 98, 99, 107, 108, 109, 111, 113, 117, 119, 120, 121, 123, 125, 126, 127
legal protection, 48
legislation, 6, 9, 20, 40, 61, 101, 120
Levant, viii, 1, 15, 16, 66, 70, 75, 88, 96
liberalism, 40
light, 50, 53, 55, 66, 72, 74, 88, 89, 92, 121
Lion, 53
logistics, 123, 125
loyalty, 17

M

major issues, 21
majority, 6, 26, 30, 49, 101, 109, 121
Malaysia, 107, 132
man, 17
management, 123, 124, 125
marketing, 22
mass, 16, 40, 103
materials, 83, 84, 127
matter, 48, 74, 75
media, 16, 37, 89, 93
mediation, 21
medical, 91, 103, 105, 106, 125, 126, 127, 133
medical assistance, 106, 125, 126
medical care, 103
medicine, 105
membership, 43
mental health, 123, 124, 126
messages, 93
Mexico, 132
Middle East, 38, 39, 66, 75, 95, 96, 98
migrants, 107
military, viii, 2, 3, 15, 17, 18, 28, 32, 39, 41, 43, 44, 46, 47, 48, 49, 50, 51, 52, 53, 67,

68, 69, 72, 76, 77, 79, 81, 85, 87, 91, 92, 97, 102, 115
military aid, 91
military exchanges, 52
militia(s), viii, 1, 6, 7, 17, 18, 19, 37, 44, 66, 68, 70, 73, 74, 79, 80, 91, 93, 96
minorities, 10, 38, 39
minority groups, 67, 106
mission(s), 7, 47, 48, 51, 52, 53, 55, 81, 82, 84, 89, 97, 135
misuse, 89
mixing, 82
momentum, 8, 102
Morocco, 111
Muslims, vii, 1, 38
mutual respect, 54

N

National Counterterrorism Center, 16
national security, 20, 25
nationalism, 41
nationality, 77
NATO, 83, 97
natural disaster(s), 120
natural gas, 35, 43
natural gas pipeline, 43
negative consequences, 85
negative effects, 72
negative outcomes, 85
negotiating, 40, 77
negotiation, 67, 74, 92
nerve, 81
Netherlands, 97, 130, 132
neutral, 41, 77, 122
New Zealand, 132
NGOs, 112, 116, 118, 119, 124, 131, 135
North Africa, ix, 99, 102, 108, 111
Norway, 84, 130, 132
nuclear program, 41, 97
nuclear talks, 40

Index

143

O

Obama, 14, 23, 31, 52, 67, 69, 81, 86, 87, 89, 98, 109, 114
Obama Administration, 14, 23, 31, 67, 69, 81, 86, 87, 89, 98, 109, 114
obstacles, 104, 116
obstruction, 69, 103, 116
OCS, 49
officials, viii, 3, 9, 16, 18, 20, 24, 25, 28, 30, 32, 35, 36, 37, 42, 43, 47, 48, 49, 52, 55, 65, 67, 68, 69, 70, 72, 75, 77, 79, 81, 84, 85, 88, 90, 91, 92, 106
oil, vii, 1, 6, 14, 21, 22, 23, 34, 35, 42, 45, 46, 49, 54, 55, 59, 62, 75, 81
oil revenues, 46
open-mindedness, 95
operations, 16, 17, 28, 44, 55, 56, 61, 68, 69, 74, 76, 82, 87, 91, 100, 104, 123, 125
opportunities, 32, 109, 127
opposition groups, viii, 42, 65, 66, 67, 68, 70, 74, 75, 76, 85, 86, 87, 88, 90, 92
organize, 6
OSC, 2, 48, 51, 52, 53, 78, 96, 97, 98
OSCE, 134
outreach, 118
oversight, 14, 36, 46, 89

P

Pakistan, 16, 134, 135
Parliament, 19
participants, 69
partition, 79
peace, 68, 77, 92, 135
peacekeeping, 92, 135
penalties, 44
permission, 43, 116
permit, 38
perpetrators, 104
Persian Gulf, 4, 40, 45, 53, 93
petroleum, 35, 75
pharmaceuticals, 126
Philadelphia, 63

pipeline, 22, 23, 45
PM, 62
PMOI, 42
Poland, 133
police, 2, 27, 30, 55
policy, 32, 43, 44, 81, 85, 87, 91, 100, 101, 102, 104, 120, 122, 133
policy choice, 104
policy issues, 101, 120
policy options, 85
polio, 106
political affiliations, 118
political conflicts, viii, 66, 72
political crisis, 22, 48
political opposition, 85
political power, 29
political system, 3
politics, vii, 4, 13, 18, 20, 24, 54
polling, 61
population, vii, viii, ix, 5, 6, 10, 11, 31, 38, 42, 65, 72, 99, 102, 103, 106, 107, 108
portfolio, 15
power sharing, 15, 19
preservation, 91
presidency, 23
president, 2, 3, 4, 5, 6, 7, 8, 14, 19, 20, 21, 24, 25, 26, 33, 41, 43, 46, 48, 52, 54, 63, 67, 68, 89, 90, 91, 95, 96, 98, 105, 122, 134
President Obama, 14, 25, 43, 46, 48, 52, 54
presidential veto, 10
prestige, 3
prevention, 103, 126
Prime Minister Nuri al-Maliki, vii, 1
principles, 66, 135
prisoners, 25, 26, 30, 31, 103
prisons, 16, 31
pro-Asad forces, viii, 66, 68, 74
procurement, 83
project, 43
proliferation, 56
proposition, 13
protection, 36, 100, 101, 102, 106, 110, 116, 118, 123, 124, 125, 126, 127, 135
provincial councils, 5, 9, 23, 29, 33

144 Index

psychosocial support, 124
public concern(s), 82
public schools, 127
public sector, 38
public service, 106
punishment, 36

R

radio, 91
rape, 103
ratification, 47
reading, 22
rebel groups, 67
recognition, 92
recommendations, 47
reconciliation, 8, 9, 45, 69, 79
reconstruction, 59, 88, 118, 122
recovery, 35, 88
reelection, 77
reform(s), 26, 27, 28, 77, 120
refugee camps, 104, 109
refugee flows, 100, 102
refugees, viii, ix, 65, 66, 72, 87, 99, 101,
    102, 103, 106, 107, 108, 109, 110, 112,
    115, 116, 117, 118, 121, 123, 124, 125,
    126, 127, 134
regulations, 9
rehabilitation, 26, 103
reintroduction, 2, 31
rejection, 8, 74, 77
relief, ix, 66, 68, 72, 100, 104, 105, 106,
    115, 117, 118, 122, 123, 124, 133
rent, 127
reporters, 82
requirements, 48
RES, 134
researchers, 26, 62
resentment, 2, 16
reserves, 35
resettlement, 22, 101, 118
resolution, 23, 46, 104, 105, 106
resources, 36, 85, 100, 102, 109, 121, 126

response, vii, 44, 67, 81, 86, 87, 89, 100,
    101, 102, 110, 111, 115, 116, 117, 118,
    119, 120, 121, 125, 126, 133, 135
response capacity, 121
restrictions, 2, 37, 56, 86, 100, 101, 102,
    116
retaliation, 80
revenue, 23, 28, 36
Revolutionary Guard, 18, 80
rhetoric, 93
rights, 36, 37, 38, 40, 74, 103
risk(s), 72, 79, 88, 98, 109, 126, 127
Romania, 133
rule of law, 33, 34, 55, 60, 89
rules, 11, 34, 38
Russia, 50, 67, 70, 83, 84, 97

S

Saddam Hussein, 2, 3, 4, 11, 15, 20, 35, 40,
    41, 56
safety, 38, 92, 115, 125
sanctions, 35, 42, 46, 56, 97
Saudi Arabia, 45, 53, 96, 98, 130, 133
school, 106, 109, 125, 127
scope, 121
Secretary of Defense, 52, 84, 90
sectarianism, 12, 36
secularism, 40, 73
security, viii, 2, 4, 6, 8, 21, 25, 27, 28, 30,
    31, 36, 37, 38, 39, 40, 44, 47, 48, 49, 51,
    52, 53, 55, 66, 69, 72, 73, 76, 82, 83, 84,
    88, 91, 92, 106, 108, 115, 123, 125
security assistance, 49, 66, 72
security forces, 2, 4, 6, 8, 28, 30, 44, 47, 49
security services, 36, 69
seizure, 86, 89
Senate, 53, 55, 85, 89-91, 96, 97, 98, 134
Senate Foreign Relations Committee, 53,
    85, 89, 90, 91, 97, 98
September 11, 132
services, 26, 37, 90, 109, 123, 124, 125,
    126, 127, 134
settlements, 76, 104, 115, 123, 124, 127
sexual violence, 103

Index

145

shape, 11, 67, 85, 104
shelter, 103, 106, 109, 115, 116, 123, 124, 125, 126, 133
Shiite factions, 45
Shiite political domination, vii, 1
Shiites, viii, 1, 7, 11, 13, 32, 38, 40, 41, 45, 46, 62
shortfall, 22
showing, 11, 24
signs, 28, 45
Slovakia, 133
social support, 125
society, 66, 70, 74
solidarity, 12, 46, 115
solution, 26, 52, 81, 86, 91, 92, 102
Somalia, 107
South Asia, 75
South Korea, 50
sovereignty, 3
Spain, 82, 130, 133
specialists, 82, 134
speech, 27, 36, 37, 95
spending, 87
stability, vii, viii, 1, 15, 40, 66, 72, 100, 102
stabilization, 9
starvation, 104
state(s), viii, 2, 4, 14, 15, 22, 36, 40, 45, 47, 53, 54, 56, 62, 66, 67, 68, 69, 73, 74, 86, 88, 91, 97
state control, viii, 66, 68
storage, 82, 83, 127
stress, 55, 85
stroke, 24, 26
structure, 3, 5, 7, 13, 15, 17, 20, 33, 51
style, 37
Sudan, 107
suicide, 7, 16
Sunni challenge, viii, 2
Sunni Muslim, vii, 1
Sunnis, 2, 6, 7, 9, 10, 11, 13, 16, 17, 19, 25, 26, 27, 28, 30, 32, 33, 43
supervision, 46, 81
support services, 125
Supreme Council, 4, 60
Supreme Court, 13, 25, 27

surveillance, 2, 31, 50
survival, 80
Sweden, 120, 130, 133
Switzerland, ix, 67, 69, 73, 95, 98, 99, 105, 130, 133
Syrian government, ix, 66, 67, 68, 69, 75, 76, 77, 79, 80, 81, 82, 83, 84, 91, 92, 99, 100, 101, 102, 105, 116, 121

T

tactics, 16, 66, 70, 73
tanks, 49
target, 28, 39, 76, 79, 85
teams, 52, 80
technical assistance, 41, 80, 84
telecommunications, 125
tension(s), 7, 21, 45, 80, 106
terminals, 35
territorial, vii, 1, 21, 73
territory, 16, 75, 82, 83
terrorism, 18, 26, 51, 52, 56, 67, 68, 69, 87, 89
terrorist attack, 106
terrorist groups, 49, 85
terrorists, 16
Thailand, 107
threat assessment, 72
threats, 18, 36, 69, 75, 85, 97
torture, 36, 103, 106
trade, 15, 56
traditions, 38
trafficking, 36
trafficking in persons, 37
training, 2, 16, 21, 31, 32, 44, 47, 49, 51, 52, 53, 55, 79, 80, 90, 98
tranches, 49
transactions, 42
translation, 96
transparency, 34, 118
transport, 83, 123, 127
transportation, 82, 83, 116
trauma, 125
Treasury, 18, 42, 58, 80, 96
treatment, 26, 38, 42, 45

146   Index

trial, 25, 45
Turkey, ix, 3, 23, 25, 42, 44, 45, 61, 62, 66,
    72, 96, 99, 107, 108, 109, 111, 113, 116,
    121, 123, 125
turnout, 13

U

U.N. Human Rights Commission, 134
U.N. Security Council, ix, 8, 46, 56, 81, 83,
    100, 104, 105, 116, 134
U.S. assistance, 54, 66, 70, 87, 92, 101, 112,
    114, 122
U.S. Department of Agriculture, 54
U.S. nonlethal assistance, viii, 65
U.S. policy, 8, 41, 42, 43, 50, 72, 85, 91,
    101, 110
U.S. Treasury, 79, 80
U.S. troop presence, 47
Ukraine, 83, 97
unions, 38
United Kingdom (UK), 83, 84, 96, 98, 129,
    133
United Nations (UN), 3, 8, 66, 67, 70, 97,
    100, 102, 103, 105, 110, 111, 113, 116,
    117, 121, 123, 124, 125, 126, 127, 128,
    129, 131, 133, 134
United Nations Development Program, 128
United Nations High Commissioner for
    Refugees (UNHCR), 107, 110, 111, 115,
    118, 123, 124, 128, 134
United Nations Industrial Development
    Organization, 129
UNRWA, 107, 117, 123, 125, 135
updating, 103
urban, 109, 118
urban areas, 118

V

vacuum, 85
vehicles, 30, 49, 50, 82, 91, 125
vessels, 84

veto, 6, 61
Vice President, 24, 25, 26, 29, 32, 45, 54
victims, 40
violence, viii, 1, 2, 7, 9, 10, 16, 20, 21, 25,
    29, 31, 32, 39, 42, 48, 69, 72, 80, 85,
    100, 101, 103, 105-109, 124, 126
violent extremist, 69
vocational education, 123
vote, viii, 2, 7, 10, 11, 13, 18, 21, 22, 23, 24,
    26, 29, 43, 47, 60, 61, 89
voters, viii, 2, 5, 6, 11, 29, 33, 61
voting, 7, 11, 32
vouchers, 126

W

waiver, 8, 36, 86
war, viii, 2, 5, 19, 27, 30, 41, 66, 72, 75, 79,
    103, 107
war crimes, 103
Washington, 5, 16, 21, 24, 25, 28, 41, 49,
    52, 61, 62, 63, 95, 96, 97, 98, 135
waste, 83
watches, 97
water, 103, 106, 109, 116, 118, 123, 124,
    125, 127
weakness, 7
weapons, ix, 10, 30, 32, 41, 52, 56, 66, 67,
    77, 79, 81, 82, 84, 85, 92, 97, 99, 102,
    103, 104, 105, 115
weapons of mass destruction, 56
wear, 40
withdrawal, vii, 1, 18, 19, 25, 41, 46, 47, 48,
    49, 54, 56, 88
workers, 38, 103, 106, 125
World Health Organization (WHO), 125,
    129
worldwide, 101, 114

Y

Yemen, 16, 43
yield, 33